A STATISTICAL ANALYSIS OF THE IRISH ELECTORAL REGISTER AND ITS USE FOR POPULATION ESTIMATION AND SAMPLE SURVEYS

GW00703373

Copies of this paper may be obtained from the Economic and Social Research Institute (Limited Company No. 18269). Registered Office: 4 Burlington Road, Dublin 4.

Price IR£6.50

(Special rate for students IR£3.25)

Gary Keogh is an Assistant Research Officer and Brendan J. Whelan is a Research Professor and Head of the Survey Unit at the Economic and Social Research Institute. The paper has been accepted for publication by the Institute, which is not responsible for either the content or the views expressed therein.

A STATISTICAL ANALYSIS OF THE IRISH ELECTORAL REGISTER AND ITS USE FOR POPULATION ESTIMATION AND SAMPLE SURVEYS

GARY KEOGH and BRENDAN J. WHELAN

© THE ECONOMIC AND SOCIAL RESEARCH INSTITUTE

DUBLIN 1986

ISBN 0 7070 0083 1

Acknowledgements

The authors would like to express their gratitude to all of the people whose help made this study possible. In particular we would like to thank Mrs E. Colbert-Stanley and the staff of the Survey Unit for the administration of the surveys on which much of this work is based. In this connection we are grateful to all those persons who participated in the surveys, especially the Registration Authorities who gave generously of their time and provided invaluable information on the Registration process. Our thanks also go to our colleagues, Denis Conniffe and Gerry Hughes, for many helpful comments and suggestions on an earlier draft of this paper. Finally, we would like to thank the clerical staff of the ESRI for typing various drafts of the paper and John Roughan and Mary McElhone for preparing the manuscript for publication. The authors are, of course, solely responsible for the final draft and any errors or omissions which remain.

CONTENTS

LIST OF TABLES

GENERAL SUMMARY

The Electoral Register's primary purpose is to serve as a list of those persons in the State who are eligible to vote in national and local elections. Apart from this function it is also used by researchers in the social sciences for other purposes, as it is the only regularly updated list of the adult population which is readily available. In particular, it has been used as a sampling frame for social surveys and as an indicator of population levels. The accuracy of the Register is, therefore, of interest to researchers.

Each year each local authority, county councils and corporations, prepares an updated copy of the Electoral Register. Following a house to house canvass in September a draft of the new Register is compiled and published on December 1st. Copies of this are made available for inspection by the public at this time and an advertising campaign is mounted to encourage people to check that they are correctly registered. Claims to have the Register amended are accepted up to January 15th and after this the definitive version of the Register is published on April 1st and comes into force on April 15th.

The present study addressed the problems of the accuracy of the Register and the extent to which any inaccuracy affects research based on the Register. There are, of course, implications of such inaccuracies for the Register as an electoral list. Our results were based on specially conducted sample surveys and historical data on the Register, going back over 30 years.

RESULTS

1. Except in the case of Dublin Borough, the registration authorities generally agreed that there had been little change in the way the Register has been compiled since 1960. A change in procedure in Dublin Borough in 1979 created a cumulating surplus of names on that Register. This surplus amounted to about 45,000 names in 1982. More recently, its effect appears to have been partially checked but not completely removed.

2. Apart from the Dublin Borough surplus most other errors of the Register would appear to be generated in the same way, by a combination of the natural flows of persons in and out of the group of people who are entitled to vote, due to persons reaching 18 years of age, deaths and persons moving, and the fact that the persons who constitute these flows are not always included in or removed from the Register at the appropriate time. Thus most of the errors of the Register are of a temporary nature.

1

3. Some 10.5 per cent of the Register in any year (in 1982 about 240,000 names) is composed of new names, of which just over a quarter are the names of persons who have recently reached 18 years of age. The remainder of this inflow is made up of people who have recently changed address. The proportion of names which is deleted every year is about 8.5 per cent (in 1981 some 194,000 names). This outflow of names corresponds to persons who have died (about 32,000 per annum) and persons who have left their previous address (some 162,000 names in 1981). The sizes of these flows indicate the magnitude of the yearly problem facing the Registration Authorities, especially as most of the persons involved are those who have left one address and arrived at another, necessitating two amendments to the Register.

4. Over 70 per cent of all persons who become eligible to be on the Register at a given place in any year are registered in that year. Most of the remainder are registered the next year but a few may have to wait two or three years to be registered. Of those who lose eligibility at a given address, because they have died or moved elsewhere, about 60 per cent are removed at the time. As with arrivals, the bulk of the outstanding errors created in this way are corrected the following year with the remainder being corrected within two or three years.

5. The errors that are created in this way lead to both deficiencies and surpluses of the Register. In any year the cumulated deficiencies of the Register arising from all earlier years amount to some 3 per cent of all persons who are entitled to vote, that is, in 1982, there were an estimated 67,000 persons who were eligible to vote but were not registered. Turnover errors also result in a surplus of about 5 per cent of the Register, which amounted to about 116,000 names in 1982. These names correspond to people who have died or left the State but who have not been deleted and people who have moved inside the State and have not been removed from the Register at their old address. When this figure is added to the Dublin surplus mentioned above the total surplus of the Register in 1982 is estimated at 157,000 names. This figure includes an estimated 128,000 names which correspond to persons who are registered twice i.e. both at their current address, and their former address.

6. As the errors of the Register are primarily created by those who are mobile they are concentrated amongst persons with certain socio-demographic characteristics. As has been found in other developed countries, this group is mainly composed of young persons and is also over-representative of those in professional and managerial occupations.

7. One advantage of an understanding of the error structure of the Register is that it is possible to make adjustments to account for these errors and obtain a set of data which reflects the numbers of persons who are actually entitled to vote. These data turn out to be more useful than those on the Register itself

when it comes to making population estimates. A statistical model for this purpose was constructed and the resulting population and migration estimates for the period 1961 to 1981 appear to be more realistic than those previously presented in Whelan and Keogh (1980). This model also embodies ideas put forward by Hughes (1981) regarding the relative times during the year to which the Register and the Census refer.

8. A second advantage of the derived data on the numbers entitled to vote is that some attempt may be made to estimate recent population levels. Using these data it appears that there may have been net immigration during the two years ending in April 1983 of about 15,000 persons. This trend has, of course, been reversed in the years since then and the subsequent migration flow is estimated to have been a net emigration of 21,000 between April 1983 and 1985. The most recently published Registers indicate a further acceleration of this trend. When account is taken of births and deaths between April 1981 and 1985 it is estimated that there were some 3,578,000 persons in the State in April 1985. This figure is 26,000 in excess of the Central Statistics Office figure of 3,552,000 for the same date. Assuming that the numbers of births and deaths across the year ending in April 1986 were approximately equal to those in the previous year it is estimated that the population in April 1986 stood at about 3,584,000.

9. A number of methods for selecting random samples of the Irish population are considered and it is shown that the Electoral Register is the only generally available listing of persons on which genuine random samples can be based. Two aspects of such samples are considered: bias and sampling error. The total bias, caused by the exclusion of some persons recently come of age and some recent movers, is estimated at 3.9 per cent of the total number of Entitled Electors. This bias is not likely to be serious except in surveys targetted specifically at young people or those most prone to move house. Two sample designs based on the Register are described and true standard errors are calculated for one of them. It is shown that the typical design effect (i.e. the ratio of the actual standard error to that of a simple random sample of the same size) lies in the range 1.5-2.0. This result gives some justification to the common practice of estimating standard errors of complex sample designs by calculating the standard error for a sample random.

10. It is estimated that some 67,000 persons (3 per cent of the Entitled Electors) should have votes but do not, while 157,000 (7 per cent of the Entitled Electors) are registered who should not be. It is clear that both types of error are undesirable: the former means that people are wrongly deprived of their votes while the latter type of errors allows for the possibility of electoral abuse in the form of personation and double voting.

11. It is suggested that the value of the Register as a research tool could be

improved if the Registration Authorites obtained information on the reason for each change of address and on the number of persons aged under 18 years in each household. Data on the gross flows onto and off the Register should be published, i.e. the total new comers of age, total arrivals onto the Register, total deletions and total deaths. This would yield valuable information on migration flows. Enhancements of the Register along these lines are being used in other countries.

12. The Electoral Register is a valuable research tool both for population estimation and sampling. It has certain deficiencies which we have documented but, for most research purposes, these are neither as serious nor as wide-spread as anecdotal evidence might suggest. The most important deficiency appears to be in Dublin surplus. In our view, it is important that this problem is rectified not only for research purposes but also because of the potential for electoral abuse which it involves.

Chapter 1

INTRODUCTION AND DESCRIPTION OF THE REGISTER

Introduction

The primary purpose of the Irish Electoral Register is to serve as a list of those persons in the State who are eligible to vote in national and local elections. However, as it is the only available list of a large proportion of the State's population, researchers in the social sciences have turned to it for other purposes: as a sampling frame for large social surveys and as an indicator of demographic changes. Given that it is used in these ways it would seem reasonable to make a statistical analysis of the Register itself since such an analysis could shed light on its strengths and weaknesses in these contexts. Thus the present study has three purposes: (i) to examine the statistical properties of the Register as a regularly updated list of persons and to quantify the extent to which it is accurate; (ii) to determine whether and how the Register can be used as a means of estimating population in years when a census is not carried out; (iii) to determine the usefulness of the Register as a frame from which samples of the population can be selected. To our knowledge, no systematic evaluation of the Register for research purposes has been published, although some relevant studies have been published in the last two areas mentioned.

We realise that not all of our readers will be interested in each of the three areas. Therefore the study has been divided into chapters which will, we hope, allow readers to find with ease those topics in which they are interested. A brief overview of the paper is now presented, together with some comments on how it relates to previous work in each of the three areas.

The second section of the present chapter provides a description of the Register and how it is compiled. Chapter 2, which attempts to model the dynamics of the Register and to estimate the magnitude of likely errors, is the cornerstone of the study since all the subsequent chapters depend on it. Here, estimates of the numbers of persons flowing onto and off the Register are given and it is shown that the errors of the Register are mostly due to delays in the registration process. Estimates of the magnitude of various types of error are provided in a variety of categories. Clearly, the magnitude and nature of such errors has implications for both the areas of research discussed above.

The use of the Electoral Register for population estimation was first discussed in Whelan and Keogh (1980). That paper presented methods based on ratios or regressions which provided estimates for the non-census years of the population for each county and county borough. These estimates were shown to be more accurate than those published by the Central Statistics

Office in the 1970s. Keenan (1981) and Hughes (1981) discussed the Whelan and Keogh estimates with particular reference to the point in time at which the Register could be considered to approximate most clearly to the total population aged 18 years and over.

The application of the original Whelan and Keogh estimating method to the years 1980 and 1981 gave unrealistically high results. In Chapter 2, below, most of this problem is traced to a change in enumeration procedure in Dublin Borough which left increasing numbers of redundant names on that Register. Appropriate corrections are suggested. With these and some other adjustments to the Register (described in Appendix A) a new and, in our view, superior estimating method is developed in Chapters 3 and 4. This new method has a number of advantages over the original one. First, it allowed us to solve the problem posed by Keenan and Hughes by means of a parameter estimated as part of our model. Secondly, it is much more parsimonious: the number of parameters to be estimated is reduced from 26 to 11. Thirdly, smooth secular trends such as changes in the age structure or even gradual changes in the registration procedure can be accommodated within the system. Estimates of population for each planning region in each year from 1961 to 1981 are presented as well as estimates of the national population for the years 1982-85.

Chapter 5 uses the results of Chapter 2 to consider the question of sample selection from the Register. Relatively little has been written on this topic in Ireland. O'Muircheartaigh and Wiggins (1977) published a description of a sample design, based on the Register, which was used in a study of social mobility. A number of other large-scale surveys also used samples derived from the Register which are described in the relevant publications, McGreil (1977), Joint National Media Research Survey (1983). The ESRI's computer based random sampling system, RANSAM, is described in Whelan (1979). Some attention has been given to deriving estimates of standard errors from samples originating in the Register, but this has, in general, been confined to assuming the validity of simple random sampling formulae, possibly multiplied by some arbitrary factor such as 1.5. Given the nature of the samples used in practice, which incorporate numerous features such as stratification and clustering, the use of such formulae is open to question. Furthermore, little information is available on the possibly more serious question of biases in the Register and consequently little attention has been paid to errors arising from such bias. Information on both these topics is provided in Chapter 5.

We discuss how the various categories of error described in Chapter 2 are likely to affect the validity of samples based on the Register. Some correct estimates of typical standard errors for a particular sample design are also presented and compared with those derived from formulae which assume simple random sampling.

An evaluation of the Register from an electoral point of view is contained in the Report of the Working Party on the Register of Electors (1982). This report, while enumerating the various types of possible error, does not present quantitative estimates of their frequency of occurrence. As our study enabled us to produce such estimates we were able to discuss the implications of these inaccuracies for elections. Our analysis of the ways in which these errors arise also allows us to make some suggestions on how they may be minimized. These matters are discussed in Chapter 6.

Description of the Register

This section of the study describes how the Irish Electoral Register is compiled and published. It is based on two sources: the Electoral Acts 1923-63, which set out the legal requirements and an informal census of all of the thirty-one registration authorities which we undertook in summer 1982 in order to determine the detailed procedures and practices employed in compiling the Register. A copy of the questionnaire which we used in conducting the latter inquiry is given in Appendix B. It can be seen that it referred to timing, staffing and methods of compilation and publication.

Purpose of the Register and Eligibility

The basic purpose of the Register is to list all those eligible to vote in three types of election: Dail (parliamentary) elections, local authority elections and European (parliamentary) elections. The register also has a function as a list of potential jurors, who may be summoned for jury duty. The 1963 Electoral Act (Section 6) states that: "A register, by reference to registration areas consisting of administrative counties and county boroughs shall be prepared and published in every year, of persons who are entitled to be registered as electors"[1]. Section 7 goes on to state that "It shall be the duty of each council of a county and corporation of a county borough to prepare and publish the Register of Electors".

The Register comprises the following three types of elector:[2]

---

[1] The 31 administrative regions referred to here comprise the four county boroughs of Dublin, Cork, Limerick and Waterford, Tipperary North Riding, Tipperary South Riding and the remaining 25 counties. For convenience we often use the term "counties" to describe all these regions elsewhere in the text. Dun Laoghaire Borough is included with Dublin county.

[2] The result of a recent referendum has empowered the Dail to extend the francise of Dail electors to persons who are not Irish citizens. However, no specific legislation had been enacted at the time of writing.

Type	Definition	Number 1984/85 Register
Dail Electors	Resident Irish citizens	2,399,257
Local Government Electors	All permanent residents	2,419,573
European Parliament Electors	All resident citizens of E.E.C. countries	2,413,404

The validity of the Register extends from April 15 of one year to April 14 of the next and all electors on the Register must be eighteen years of age or over on the date it comes into force. The legal criteria for admission to the Register also require that electors were usually resident at the address at which they are registered on September 15 of the year before that to which the Register refers. Members of the Defence Forces and Gardai are entitled to a postal vote and their names carry the suffix P in the Register.

Method of Compilation

The Register is compiled and published annually by each of the 31 Local Authorities specified in the Act. In September of each year each registration authority organizes a house-to-house canvass of its area. This is usually carried out by rate collectors, rent collectors or other permanent employees of the Local Authority. In some areas, however, the Register inspectors are specially recruited temporary employees. In carrying out the operation the inspectors are permitted to take information from neighbours or others if they are satisfied with its accuracy and if they cannot contact the residents of a particular address. If information is not available from either of these sources, the inspector leaves a claim form which the household is asked to return by post. A copy of the claim form is shown in Appendix D. In practice, especially in rural areas, the inspector is often well acquainted with the residents of the area and has detailed local information about deaths, moves and coming of age. In our survey we were told that some inspectors keep records of deaths as published in local newspapers and in other areas information on deaths was obtained from the Registrar of Births, Deaths and Marriages.

The information collected during this canvass is then collated by the Local Authority in the form of a draft Register which is published on December 1. Copies are sent to Garda stations, Post Offices, Dispensaries, etc. and an advertising campaign is mounted to encourage members of the public to check that they are accurately registered. Anyone whose name is omitted from the Register, or who desires to have some alteration made on the Register, submits a claim form as shown in Appendix D. Such claims are accepted up to January 15 (somewhat later in some counties) and are considered by the County Registrar at a *court* usually held in February. This leads to the definitive Register which is published on April 1 and comes into force on April 15. This sequence of events is summarized in Table 1.1

Table 1.1: *Schedule for the compilation of the Register*

15 September	Final day to satisfy residence criterion
1 December	Publication of the draft Register.
15 January	Final day for the submission of claims.
1 April	Publication of Register.
15 April	Register comes into effect for 1 year.

As can be seen from Appendix B, our survey requested information on the number and sources of claims. Expressing the numbers of claims reported as percentages of the numbers on the Register in each county, the highest volume of claims encountered was just over 10 per cent. However, about three quarters of the registration authorities reported figures equivalent to less than 3 per cent of the numbers on the Register in their areas and indeed about one third of the figures reported were equivalent to less than 1 per cent. The claims were mostly reported as being made by the inspectors themselves and members of political parties: sixteen registration authorities mentioned the former source and thirteen mentioned the latter. Only eight registration authorities mentioned any other source, namely, private individuals and the gardai. All but two of the registration authorities noted that impending elections affected the number of claims made (mostly by political parties), and five registration authorities pointed out that sometimes, after elections, individuals who had discovered they were not on the Register made arrangements to be included on the next Register. However, it is difficult to gauge the effect of elections on the Register for a number of reasons. First, in order for an impending election to affect the Register it must be anticipated. Secondly, the volume of claims made in a given year is not necessarily indicative of the turnover of persons on the Register, since not all claims are allowed[3]. Thirdly, many of the persons who would have been alerted to the fact that they were not registered would have been registered the following year in any case (see Chapter 2).

We also inquired about any changes which had taken place in the method of compilation since 1960. Only in Dublin Borough and Galway was any substantial change reported. Since 1979, the Dublin Registration officers were instructed contrary to their previous practice, to leave on the Register those about whom no definite information was available. This has led to a sharp rise in the number of persons registered in Dublin City at a time when the population of the area was falling, as recorded in the Censuses of 1979 and 1981. In Galway, a court ruling in 1980 on a case brought by the student population of the city established their right to be recorded on the Register, despite the fact that many of them are elsewhere on the qualifying date. In previous years some students were allowed on to the Register on a year to year basis, applying each year at the time of claims and being subject to deletion the following year. Nowadays, students are effectively treated as full-time residents and are less likely to be deleted when they change residence. Since many of them do so, there is considerable risk of double registration. However, as there were less than 4,000 full-time students at the university in 1983, this change of practice could have only a limited effect.

Layout of the Register

The structure of the Register is determined by the "polling scheme" which is drawn up by the Local Authority and approved by the Department of the Environment. This defines the set of townlands which constitute each polling district or "book" of the Register. Townlands are combined to form books on the basis of geographical convenience to the polling stations, often a national school, used at election time. Books vary in population from a few electors to over 12,000. Within each polling district, electors are arranged by address, i.e., in towns, by street and number, in rural areas by townland. It should be noted that in some rural areas the electors are listed in alphabetical order within townland so that it is not possible to identify individual households. Each elector is allocated an elector's number starting at 1 and running up to n, where n is the number of persons in the polling district.

For survey purposes one major problem which arises with the polling districts is that in most cases maps of these districts are not published. Thus, the polling districts can only be located approximately on maps of the District Electoral Divisions.

Our survey allowed us to ascertain that nine of the thirty-one Local Authorities have computerized the Register. Clearly, sample selection would be facilitated if the complete Register was computerized in a compatible

---

[3]Indeed, since some registration authorities pointed to the political parties as the primary source of claims the number of claims may really reflect the levels of activity amongst local party members.

manner, since one could then generate lists of names and addresses for sampling purposes directly from the computer file. However, not all the Local Authorities have computerized the Register and even among those who have, it has not been done in a completely compatible manner in each county. In most places the machine used is an ICL 2903 with a COBOL program, but some authorities have other machines, such as IBM and Nixdorf. Seven Local Authorities reported that they expected their Registers to be computerized in the near future. However, it seems unlikely that direct sample selection by computer will be feasible for some considerable time, especially when one considers that the cost of purchasing the complete Register was only £236.67 in 1982.

Chapter 2

ENTRY AND EXIT PATTERNS OF THE REGISTER

Introduction

The efficacy of the Register as a sampling frame and in the context of population estimation depends on the extent to which it is accurate. In this chapter we examine this issue by estimating the extent of inaccuracies such as omissions, double registrations, deceased persons still on the Register and so on. We must begin by making a distinction between two different populations which we place under scrutiny: the Register itself, which is a published list of names and addresses; and the theoretical population of those individuals who are entitled, by the criteria described in the previous chapter, to be on the Register at a given place in a given year. For convenience, the latter population will be referred to as the population of Entitled Electors. Note that, while it is possible to define this population, in practice its members cannot be precisely listed, since they are not known. Divergences between the two populations indicate inaccuracies of the Register, whereas if the two populations coincided exactly the Register would be completely accurate. For instance, if an individual appears on the Register two or more times, at different addresses, these separate recordings of the individual constitute as many distinct elements of the Register, whereas the individual himself constitutes only one element of the population of Entitled Electors. Likewise, a deceased person whose name still appears on the Register constitutes an element of the Register, but he or she is not an Entitled Elector. For the purposes of this study, and in keeping with the legal criteria set out in Chapter 1, we shall generally consider the number of Entitled Electors to refer to the number on the 15th of September of any year in question, which is the same date as that to which the Register refers.

Our strategy for estimating the numbers of inaccuracies of the Register, i.e., the discrepancies between the two populations defined above, is based on two ideas. The first is that most errors of the Register arise as a result of changes in the population of Entitled Electors. The second is that some time may elapse before a change in the Entitled Electors is appropriately recorded on the Register. During this period the Register is in error. Thus the number of errors of the Register will depend on the extent to which the population of Entitled Electors changes from year to year, the probability that any given change gives rise to an eror, and the average amount of time for which such an error is outstanding. We also consider the possibility of errors arising in other ways but find that nearly all errors of the Register appear to be due to the causes outlined above. Thus we shall begin, in the second section of this chapter, by attempting to estimate the magnitude of yearly inflows to and outflows from the population of Entitled Electors. It will be shown that these inflows and outflows of persons may be approximated, to a degree acceptable for the purposes of this chapter, by corresponding flows of names on and off the Register. This is possible, despite the fact that the two populations are composed of differing elements. We shall refer to such flows, of both Entitled Electors and names on the Register, as gross flows to distinguish them from net flows, by which we shall mean the net change, in the size of either population, from year to year. Note that the difference between the gross inflow and the gross outflow over a year for either population is equal to the net flow of that population.

In the third section of the chapter we attempt to describe the lags that exist between changes that occur in the population of Entitled Electors and the appropriate adjustments to the Register. The various inflows and outflows to and from this population are classified by type, e.g., young people reaching 18 years of age, deaths, etc., and a statistical distribution for the delay times between each of these types of event and the times they are recorded is estimated. If there is no delay in registering an event, no error ensues. If there is a delay of one year between an event and the appropriate amendment to the Register, then an error of the Register is in existence for one year and so on. Using these estimated delay time distributions together with our estimates of the gross flows of persons who may create errors, the fourth section of this chapter makes estimates of the inaccuracies of the Register due to each type of turnover.

From the outset it was necessary to deal with the problem of the Dublin County Borough Register mentioned in Chapter 1. It will be recalled that this problem arose from a change of procedure in 1979 which left on the Register a large amount of "dead wood" in the form of listed persons no longer resident at the stated address. As a result this Register splits into two components: an active Register with properties similar to Registers in other areas; and a stockpile of names which is not updated in the same way as other Registers. Initially we adjusted the figures for Dublin County Borough by a simple smoothing method, the details of which are given in Appendix A, Section D. This allows us to split the numbers on this Register in the years 1979 to 1982 into the numbers of names which would have appeared on the Register if no change in procedure had occurred, i.e., the active Register, and the stockpile of names. The figures for the active Register are used when our estimates of both the flow rates and the errors of the Register are made in the earlier sections of the chapter. We must do this since the measured total flows of names on to the Dublin Borough Register were artifically inflated during the time period in question and hence were not generated by a mechanism similar to that operating elsewhere in the State. Our argument depends on the uniformity of this mechanism across the different Registration areas. However, in the fifth section of the present chapter the Dublin stockpile is examined in detail and the errors that arise from it are computed. These are added to our earlier estimates of the turnover errors of the Register to give estimates of the errors of the Register as a whole. This section also briefly deals with the geographical location of the stockpile within the Borough area. Although this analysis is of interest in itself, more importantly, it confirms that the stockpile is mainly in the areas one would expect it to be if it were formed in the manner described in Chapter 1.

Samples of persons drawn from the Register for survey purposes are usually drawn in the belief that the Register is representative of the population aged 18 years and over, that is, the population of Entitled Electors. To the extent that the Register is in error, this is not true. In particular, the fact that the Register is inaccurate means that some groups of individuals may be over- or under-represented. For this reason, in the final section of the Chapter, we attempt to give some indication of the socio-demographic features of the individuals who create registration errors. They break into three main sub-groups: those who have recently reached the age of franchise, those who are recently deceased and internal and external migrants. The demographic features of these groups are described using a number of standard classifications. We also consider the reasons for mobility and the extent to which mobile persons cross registration area boundaries.

The analyses outlined in this Chapter were based on specially conducted sample surveys which are described below. However, at each stage of our analysis it is possible to compare at least some figure derived from the surveys with census data, and this is done with confirmatory results.

Gross Flows of Entitled Electors

Our objective in this section is to estimate the size of the various gross flows into and out of the Entitled Electors. We begin by showing that the sizes of these flows can be approximated by the corresponding flows of names onto and from the Register itself when certain conditions hold. Although we can subsequently verify that these conditions do hold, it is convenient, to facilitate a clear presentation of our results, to begin by treating them as assumptions to be confirmed at a later stage in the Chapter. The necessary assumptions are as follows. First, we must assume that the gross flows of persons into and out of the Entitled Electors change slowly in size from year to year. Secondly, we must assume that the structure of the lags that exist between changes in the population of Entitled Electors and the corresponding adjustments to the Register stays reasonably constant over time and that these lags are generally quite short. In particular we must assume that, at any point in time, most of the errors of the current Register originate from fairly recent changes amongst the Entitled Electors. Equivalently, we are assuming that there are very few errors of the Register outstanding as a result of events which took place more than a few years prior to the current registration year, and that eventually all errors of the Register are corrected.

To formalize the ideas in the last paragraph we shall start with the case of inflows. For a fixed (current) year t let F_t be the total inflow of names onto the Register of year t, that is, the total number of names appearing at given addresses which did not appear at those addresses during the previous registration year, $t-1$. Note that, as we are concerned with names at specific addresses, the possibility that an individual's name simultaneously appears at some other address does not prevent that name from being part of the inflow. For s = 0, 1, 2 . . . and so on, let X_{t-s} be the total flow of individuals into the Entitled Electors in year $t-s$, that is, the year s years prior to the current year. The reader will recall that as Entitled Electors are defined to be at a given place at a given time, a person moving within the State, constitutes both part of the inflow to, and part of the outflow from, the Entitled Electors for that year. Persons reaching the age of franchise and immigrants from abroad form the remainder of the inflow. Let p_s be the proportion of this flow of individuals (from year $t-s$) who become registered in the current registration year. Then the total inflow into the Register, F_t, may be written:

$$F_t = p_0 X_t + p_1 X_{t-1} + p_2 X_{t-2} + \dots \tag{2.1}$$

Thus, the current inflow of names into the Register is made up of persons who are registered immediately on arrival at a new address or on entry into the Entitled Electors, persons who have waited one year to be registered and so on. Our assumption of the constancy of the lag structure implies that the coefficients p_0, p_0, p_1, p_2 . . . etc. stay constant from year to year, and our assumption that all persons with a right to vote are eventually registered implies that the proportions sum to unity, i.e. $\sum_{s=0}^{\infty} p_s = 1$. We also expect this sequence is rapidly declining as we imagine that most persons become registered relatively quickly, say within a maximum of 4 or 5 years. In other words for some small value of r, $\sum_{s=r}^{\infty} p_s$ is very small. Now if the sizes of the inflows of Entitled Electors change slowly from year to year then we may take X_t as an approximation to X_{t-s} for low values of s, say for values of s less than r.

Hence:

$$F_t \doteqdot p_0 X_t + p_1 X_{t-1} + \dots + p_{r-1} X_{t-r+1} + \sum_{s=r}^{\infty} p_s X_{t-s} \tag{2.2}$$
$$\doteqdot (p_0 + p_1 + \dots + p_{r-1}) X_t + \sum_{s=r}^{\infty} p_s X_{t-s}$$
$$\doteqdot X_t$$

$$\text{since } \sum_{s=0}^{r-1} p_s = \sum_{s=0}^{\infty} p_s - \sum_{s=r}^{\infty} p_s = 1 - \sum_{s=r}^{\infty} p_s \doteq 1$$

$$\text{and } \sum_{s=r}^{\infty} p_s X_{t-s} \doteq 0,$$

the latter approximation holding because $\sum_{s=r}^{\infty} p_s$ is very small and clearly the sequence X_{t-s} must be bounded from above.

So we have demonstrated that the number of names flowing onto the Register is approximately equal to the numbers of persons flowing into the Entitled Electors, despite the fact that these names and persons do not necessarily correspond. A similar analyses shows that the outflows from the Entitled Electors may be approximated by the outflows from the Register.

In order to derive numerical estimates of the gross flows, we selected two samples of individuals from the Register as follows[4].

(i) A random sample of 5,000 names was selected from the 1982/83 Register and those names which did not appear on the 1981/82 Register (at the same address) were noted.

(ii) Similarly a sample from the 1981/82 Register was checked against the 1982/83 Register. The sample size here was 5,130.

The first sample yielded a set of 533 names which had arrived onto the Register; the second sample produced a set of 435 names which had been removed from the Register. Accordingly, initial estimates of the numbers of new names on the 1982/83 Register in each county could be obtained by multiplying the total figure for the numbers on that county's Register by the proportion of new names as estimated from the sample. Likewise, using the total figures for the 1981/82 Register, estimates of the total numbers of deleted names in each county could be obtained. The numbers on the Register in both years, the estimated percentages of new elements of the 1982/83 Register and of deleted elements of the 1981/82 Register together with the corresponding gross flow figures are given in Table 2.1. The initial estimate of the overall rate of inflow is just over 10.5 per cent and that of the outflow amounts to 8.5 per cent. The magnitude of these flows emphasises the difficulty of the task facing the Registration Authorities in trying to keep the Register up to date.

It was possible to check and refine these estimates of gross flows by virtue of the fact that the aggregate net flows between the registration years 1981/82 and 1982/83 are known. This provided an additional constraint on the estimates

[4]Both samples were selected using the RAMSAM system as described in Chapter 5. RANSAM generates cluster samples, stratified by county, the clusters being selected with probability proportional to size. In this application a minimum cluster size of 200 persons was set and 10 individuals were selected from each cluster.

Table 2.1 *Numbers of persons on the Register in each county in the registration years 1981/ 82 and 1982/83 together with the initial estimates of the flows out of and into these Registers respectively given in gross and as percentages.*

	Register 1981/82	Outflow		Register 1982/83	Inflow	
		Persons	%		Persons	%
CORK BOROUGH	87,095	8,709	10.0	89,627	12,265	13.7
DUBLIN BOROUGH	351,562*	40,535	11.5	347,516*	44,204	12.7
LIMERICK BOROUGH	38,798	2,910	7.5	39,496	4,388	11.1
WATERFORD BOROUGH	24,164	2,416	10.0	24,440	2,933	12.0
CARLOW	25,828	2,583	10.0	26,848	2,148	8.0
CAVAN	38,761	431	1.1	39,057	2,604	6.7
CLARE	59,229	2,734	4.6	60,902	6,559	10.8
CORK	175,959	14,889	8.5	179,536	18,426	10.3
DONEGAL	85,875	7,684	9.0	86,986	7,732	8.9
DUBLIN	282,269	22,493	8.0	297,387	31,541	10.6
GALWAY	117,526	4,788	4.1	122,420	15,067	12.3
KERRY	85,445	7,195	8.4	85,723	5,715	6.7
KILDARE	64,235	3,854	6.0	68,311	6,343	9.3
KILKENNY	46,563	4,656	10.0	47,480	4,748	10.0
LAOIS	32,895	1,880	5.7	33,458	5,258	15.7
LEITRIM	20,691	2,069	10.0	20,709	1,243	6.0
LIMERICK	66,637	7,108	10.7	69,223	6,428	9.3
LONGFORD	21,158	1,693	8.0	21,416	1,606	7.5
LOUTH	57,503	4,866	8.5	58,867	10,868	18.5
MAYO	83,472	4,833	5.8	83,362	6,947	8.8
MEATH	61,817	5,740	9.3	63,623	6,362	10.0
MONAGHAN	34,935	3,057	8.8	35,501	3,043	8.6
OFFALY	37,685	2,355	6.3	38,680	4,351	11.3
ROSCOMMON	37,722	3,301	8.8	38,160	4,770	12.5
SLIGO	38,079	5,712	15.0	38,975	4,385	11.3
TIPPERARY N.R.	39,817	5,176	13.0	40,137	2,007	5.0
TIPPERARY S.R.	50,796	5,080	10.0	51,744	3,622	7.0
WATERFORD	33,614	1,867	5.6	34,412	4,301	12.5
WESTMEATH	39,947	3,551	8.9	40,740	5,885	14.4
WEXFORD	65,126	3,039	4.7	66,852	4,775	7.1
WICKLOW	56,547	3,770	6.7	58,731	4,518	7.7
STATE	2,261,750	192,023**	8.5	2,310,319	246,049**	10.7

*These are the values of the Dublin Register after the adjustments outlined in Appendix A have been made.
**These figures were obtained by treating the State as a single region; hence they differ marginally from the column totals.

which may be defined as follows. If, in any county, the true proportions of names on the 1981/82 Register which were deleted and of names on the 1982/83 Register, which are new, are denoted a and b respectively, the following identity must hold

$$R_{82} = R_{81} - aR_{81} + bR_{82} \tag{2.3}$$

where R_{81} and R_{82} denote the numbers of names on the 1981/82 and 1982/83 Registers. Equivalently:

$$R_{82} - R_{81} = bR_{82} - aR_{81}, \tag{2.4}$$

and the figure on the left hand side of this equation is known.

Now if $\hat{a}$ and $\hat{b}$ represent the corresponding proportions estimated from the sample it follows that an estimate of the net change in the size of the Register, $(R_{82} - R_{81})$, is given by $\hat{b}R_{82} - \hat{a}R_{81}$.

If $\hat{a}$ and $\hat{b}$ are unbiased estimates of a and b respectively then the random variable defined as $\hat{a} - g\hat{b} - c$, where $g = R_{82}/R_{81}$ and $c = (R_{81} - R_{82})/R_{81}$, will have an expectation of zero. Furthermore, since the samples used to calculate $\hat{a}$ and $\hat{b}$ were independent, the variance of this random variable is:

$$\text{Var} (\hat{a} - g\hat{b} - c) = \text{Var} (\hat{a}) + g^2 \text{Var} (\hat{b})$$

Thus if:

$$p = (\hat{a} - g\hat{b} - c)/[\text{Var}(\hat{a}) + g^2 \text{Var} (\hat{b})]^{\frac{1}{2}}$$

it follows that $E(p) = 0$ and $\text{Var} (p) = 1$,

and, as $\hat{a}$ and $\hat{b}$ are sample proportions, $\text{Var} (\hat{a})$ and $\text{Var} (\hat{b})$ may be estimated by the usual formula[5].

The mean and variance of p estimated across counties were -0.044 and 1.151 respectively yielding a t statistic of -0.228 which is far from being significantly different from zero. Thus we have reasonable evidence that the process of looking up names sampled from one Register on another Register had not introduced any bias into the estimates of a and b.

Our introduction of the constraint (2.3) above serves another important purpose. It may be used to improve our estimates of a and b. Equation 2.3 may be rewritten as $b = (a-c)/g$ where c and g are as previously defined. Thus a second, independent and unbiased estimate of b is given by:

$$\hat{b} = (\hat{a}-c)/g.$$

Note that $\text{Var} (\hat{b}) = \text{Var} (\hat{a})/g^2$. If:

$$W_a = 1/\text{Var} (\hat{a}) \text{ and } W_b = 1/\text{Var} (\hat{b})$$

[5]The variance of a is estimated by Var (a) = a (1-a)/n where n is the county sample size. As the clusters were small the clustering effect was ignored.

Table 2.2 *Refined estimates of the flows out of the 1981/82 Register and into the 1982/83 Register given as percentages and in gross.*

	Percentage Outflow = 100 a*	Total Outflow = a*R_{81}	Percentage Inflow = 100 b*	Total Inflow = b*R_{82}
CORK BOROUGH	11.1	9,710	13.7	12,242
DUBLIN BOROUGH	13.7	48,082	12.7	44,036
LIMERICK BOROUGH	9.5	3,670	11.1	4,368
WATERFORD BOROUGH	11.0	2,653	12.0	2,929
CARLOW	4.5	1,163	8.1	2,183
CAVAN	5.2	1,997	5.9	2,293
CLARE	8.1	4,792	10.6	6,465
CORK	8.4	14,850	10.3	18,427
DONEGAL	7.7	6,647	8.9	7,758
DUBLIN	5.9	16,595	10.7	31,713
GALWAY	8.4	9,899	12.1	14,793
KERRY	6.4	5,483	6.7	5,761
KILDARE	3.6	2,328	9.4	6,404
KILKENNY	8.3	3,850	10.0	4,767
LAOIS	14.0	4,602	15.4	5,165
LEITRIM	6.0	1,245	6.1	1,263
LIMERICK	5.9	3,913	9.4	6,499
LONGFORD	6.4	1,358	7.5	1,616
LOUTH	16.3	9,393	18.3	10,757
MAYO	8.4	6,975	8.2	6,865
MEATH	7.4	4,585	10.0	6,391
MONAGHAN	7.1	2,492	8.6	3,058
OFFALY	8.8	3,324	11.2	4,320
ROSCOMMON	11.4	4,308	12.4	4,746
SLIGO	9.2	3,521	11.3	4,417
TIPPERARY N.R.	4.4	1,760	5.2	2,080
TIPPERARY S.R.	5.4	2,723	7.1	3,671
WATERFORD	10.2	3,432	12.3	4,230
WESTMEATH	12.7	5,055	14.4	5,848
WEXFORD	4.7	3,049	7.1	4,775
WICKLOW	4.2	2,379	7.8	4,563
STATE	8.6	193,832[1]	10.5	242,583[1]
95% CONFIDENCE INTERVAL				
LOWER BOUND	8.0	180,940	9.9	228,722
UPPER BOUND	9.2	208,081	11.1	256,215

[1] These figures were obtined by treating the State as a single region, hence they differ marginally from the column totals.

then the usual rule for combining two independent estimates of the same parameter in proportion to the reciprocals of their variances yields, on simplification:

$$b^* = (g\,W_a(\hat{a} - c) + W_b\hat{b})/(g^2 W_a + W_b) \qquad (2.5)$$

This in turn yields a new estimate of a, via the constraint, of:

$$a^* = gb^* + c \qquad (2.6)$$

Because these estimates are derived from the pooled information contained in both samples, their variances are substantially lower than those of $\hat{a}$ and $\hat{b}$. Indeed:

$$\mathrm{Var}\,(b^*) = 1/(g^2 W_a + W_b)$$

$$\mathrm{Var}\,(a^*) = g^2\,\mathrm{Var}\,(b^*)$$

and when these formulae were used (with $\mathrm{Var}\,(\hat{a})$ and $\mathrm{Var}\,(\hat{b})$ as calculated using the usual formula in W_a and W_b) we found that the associated standard deviations, and hence confidence intervals for a^* and b^*, were 25 per cent to 35 per cent smaller than those for $\hat{a}$ and $\hat{b}$.

These estimates of a and b for each county are given in Table 2.2 along with the corresponding new estimates of the gross flows. This table also gives confidence intervals for these proportions and gross flows for the case of the State as a whole. As can be seen from this table the estimates for the State as a whole have been changed only slightly[6], due to the fact that $\hat{a}$ and $\hat{b}$ were already close estimates of a and b. However, for some counties the estimates have changed markedly. This is to be expected since some of these estimates were based on fairly small samples and thus would have naturally large variances.

Our next task was to separate the gross flows into their various components. The inflows were separated, for each county, into the group who had arrived onto the Register as a result of reaching the age of franchise and immigrants; the outflows were expressed as the sums of deaths and emigrants. The numbers reaching the age of franchise in April 1982 were estimated by taking the numbers aged 15 years in each county, as reported in Vol. II of the 1979 Census of Population, and using the most recent Irish Life tables (Statistical Abstract 1976) to age this cohort. This amounted to multiplying the figures by 0.9982. The numbers of deaths in each county were obtained from the Central Statistics Office Quarterly Report on Births, Deaths and Marriages. These figures were then multiplied by a factor of 0.9605, which is the

---

[6]Although the estimates for the State have changed only slightly this does not make this exercise pointless. We can now have greater confidence in our results.

proportion of all deaths which are amongst those aged 18 years and over for the State as a whole. The reader will notice that we are again employing our hypothesis regarding the approximate equality of flows of persons into and out of the Entitled Electors and the corresponding flows of names to and from the Register. Also we are ignoring certain fringe effects, such as net migration amongst those aged 18 years. Such effects are slight in comparison to the sizes of the flows under consideration and are certainly well within the bounds of accuracy to which we are working. Estimates of the numbers of immigrants and emigrants to and from the Register were obtained as residuals to the numbers reaching the age of franchise and the numbers of deaths. All these estimates are given in gross and as percentages in Table 2.3.

The table shows that about a quarter of the flow into the Register is constituted by persons reaching the age of franchise, the remaining three quarters being composed of immigrants. Deaths account for just over 16 per cent of the outflow, the remainder are emigrants. Of course, most of the flows of the Register in the two categories of migrants correspond to the same individuals who have been recorded as having left one place and arrived at another. Indeed many might be better labelled as 'mobile' rather than 'migratory' since the latter description is usually reserved for individuals who, when moving, cross some prespecified boundary. As this distinction is not germane to the contents of this chapter, we shall continue to refer to all mobile individuals as migrants.

It is instructive to compare the estimates of the gross inflow and the number of immigrants in 1982 with corresponding figures which may be estimated from the 1971 Census of Population. Volume XI of the 1971 census gives figures for the numbers of persons living at the same or a different address in April 1971 as compared with April 1970. The relevant breakdown of the usually resident population given in the Census is presented in Table 2.4.

We need three further figures to construct the required estimates of the gross flows onto the (adjusted) Register in 1971[7].

1. Total (adjusted) Register 1971	1,944,640
2. Persons aged 18 years in 1971	52,665
3. Persons aged 18 years in 1971 at a different address to 1 year previously[8]	2,893

---

[7] As explained in Appendix A, section C, it is necessary to adjust the Register for the years prior to 1972/73 to allow for the change in voting age. As this has been done it is appropriate to use breakdowns based on those under 18 years and those aged 18 years and over.

[8] One fifth of the corresponding group aged 15 to 19 years.

Table 2.3: *Deaths amongst those aged 18 years and over during the registration year September 1980 to September 1981, 18 year olds at September 1981, together with the implied estimates of emigrants out of and immigrants onto the 1981/82 and 1982/83 Registers respectively given in gross and in percentage terms.*

	Deaths *(18 and over)*	*Emigrants* *Persons*	*%*	*18 year olds*	*Immigrants* *Persons*	*%*
CORK BOROUGH	1,294	8,416	9.7	3,029	9,214	10.3
DUBLIN BOROUGH	5,286	42,796	12.2	11,577	32,456	9.3
LIMERICK BOROUGH	448	3,222	8.3	1,448	2,920	7.4
WATERFORD BOROUGH	354	2,298	9.5	780	2,149	8.8
CARLOW	375	788	3.1	826	1,357	5.1
CAVAN	588	1,409	3.6	1,017	1,275	3.3
CLARE	860	3,932	6.6	1,502	4,962	8.1
CORK	2,612	12,238	7.0	4,844	13,583	7.6
DONEGAL	1,368	5,279	6.1	2,333	5,425	6.2
DUBLIN	2,291	14,304	5.1	8,455	23,258	7.8
GALWAY	1,695	8,203	7.0	3,408	11,385	9.3
KERRY	1,426	4,057	4.7	2,249	3,512	4..1
KILDARE	703	1,625	2.5	1,106	5,298	7.8
KILKENNY	669	3,182	6.8	1,354	3,414	7.2
LAOIS	474	4,129	12.6	1,084	4,081	12.2
LEITRIM	464	781	3.8	494	769	3.7
LIMERICK	816	3,097	4.6	1,806	4,693	6.8
LONGFORD	373	986	4.7	620	996	4.7
LOUTH	774	8,619	15.0	1,703	9,055	15.4
MAYO	1,442	5,533	6.6	2,216	4,649	5.6
MEATH	741	3,845	6.2	1,839	4,552	7.2
MONAGHAN	525	1,967	5.6	970	2,088	5.9
OFFALY	516	2,809	7.5	1,366	2,954	7.6
ROSCOMMON	706	3,602	9.5	1,076	3,670	9.6
SLIGO	685	2,837	7.4	1,090	3,327	8.5
TIPPERARY N.R.	605	1,154	2.9	1,183	897	2.2
TIPPERARY S.R.	784	1,939	3.8	1,613	2,058	4.0
WATERFORD	527	2,905	8.6	1,124	3,106	9.0
WESTMEATH	582	4,473	11.2	1,291	4,557	11.2
WEXFORD	939	2,109	3.2	1,927	2,848	4.3
WICKLOW	758	1,621	2.9	1,613	2,950	5.0
STATE	31,677[1]	162,155[2]	7.2	66,940[1]	175,643[2]	7.6

[1]Figures differ from column totals due to rounding.
[2]These figures were obtained by treating the State as a single region, hence they differ marginally from the column totals.

Table 2.4: *Persons usually resident in the State aged 1 to 17 years and aged 18 years and over in 1971 broken down by address one year previously.*

| Age Group | Address 1 year previously | | Total |
	Same Address	Different Address	
1-17	979,602	43,054	1,022,656
18 and over	1,765,222	105,293	1,870,515
All ages*	2,744,824	148,348	2,893,172

*Columns do not add exactly due to rounding.

From these figures and the figures in Table 2.4 we may estimate the number of persons expected to arrive onto the (adjusted) 1971/72 Register as:

155,065 = 105,293   (as a result of migration)
      +   52,665   (those reaching the age of franchise)
      −   2,893   (migrants who also reached the age of franchise)

i.e., about 8 per cent of the 1971/72 Register[9]. Compared with our estimated inflow of 242,583 in 1982 we see that the size of the gross inflow onto the Register has grown by a factor of 1.554 (= 242,583/156,065), an average growth rate over the 11 intervening years of 4.1 per cent per annum. When the same calculation is performed for immigrants alone, the annual growth rate of this flow size is seen to be 4.8 per cent ($(175,643/105,293)^{1/11} = 1.048$). These figures indicate that the growth rates of the flows onto the Register are sufficiently small that, to the extent that the approximation technique described in equation (2.2) depends on this fact, they are adequate. Of course, strictly speaking, we have in fact used this approximating technique in the very construction of the above figures, since they estimate flows of the Entitled Electors. But the notion that the flow sizes of the Entitled Electors could sustain a long run growth rate significantly different from those of the Register seems extremely unlikely, as such discrepancies over the long run would have to lead to large and glaring differences between the two populations. In any case, Bulletin 41 of the 1981 Census of Population reports 205,048 persons usually resident in the State aged 1 year and over who were at a different address to 1 year previously, and, when this is compared to the corresponding figure of 148,348 persons from the 1971 Census we see that this flow had risen

[9]These figures represent April to April flows, but it is unlikely that the September to September flows (1969 to 1970) differ by appreciable amounts.

on average at a rate of 3.3 per cent per annum over the ten years. This figure is not directly comparable with the figures for the sizes of the inflows of the Entitled Electors, since it includes all age groups. Nevertheless it further confirms the fact that these flows are changing slowly.

We may also estimate the outflow from the (adjusted) 1970/71 Register using the definitional fact that:

$$\text{OUTFLOW} = \text{INFLOW} - \text{NET FLOW}$$
$$= \text{INFLOW} - (R_{71} - R_{70})$$
$$= 155,065 - 15,674$$
$$= 139,391$$

which is 7.3 per cent of the 1970/71 Register. As the number of deaths in that year should have accounted for 30,192 elements of the outflow, the number of immigrants is seen to be 110,199. When these two figures are compared with our outflow figures for 1981/82 it appears that both these flows have grown at rates of less than 4 per cent per annum.

Our final observations on gross flows concerns those names which were both entered onto and deleted from the 1982/83 Register. Of the 533 names identified in our first sample as having arrived on to the 1982/83 Register, it was possible to determine with certainty the status of 525 of them vis a vis the 1983/84 Register. Some 99 of these names were no longer recorded at the addresses where they were found in the sample, i.e. nearly 19 per cent. The outflow rate for the Register as a whole is about 8.5 per cent. Thus the conditional probability of a name being deleted from the Register, given that it had just been entered, is just double the unconditional probabilty of a name being deleted. Deaths are likely to account for proportionally less of this outflow than for the Register as a whole, because, as we shall show later in this chapter, movers tend to be concentrated in lower age groups. Also, as those reaching the age of franchise only constitute about one quarter of the total inflow, the phenomenon of persons arriving onto the Register by dint of coming of age and then moving out of home cannot explain the greatly increased rate of outflow amongst newly registered names. Thus we are led to the view that among the mobile population there is a substantial number of chronic movers, i.e., persons with a high rate of turnover in addresses. Such persons will obviously cause particular difficulties for the Registration authorities.

Details of the numbers of names which were identified both as arrivals and as departures from the 1982/83 Register, along with the corresponding conditional outflow rates, are given for each planning region in Table 2.5 (the numbers were too small for useful disaggregation by county). It can be seen from the table that apart from the North West and Donegal, where in any case

Table 2.5: *Numbers of persons identified as arrivals onto and as departures from the 1982/ 83 Register together with total arrivals and the corresponding percentage figures.*

Planning Region	Removed Persons	Total Persons	Removed/ Total x 100 %
East	40	206	19.42
South West	14	77	18.18
South East	9	46	19.57
North East	10	35	22.22
Mid-West	7	39	17.95
Midlands	8	46	17.39
West	9	48	18.75
North West and Donegal	2	28	7.14
State	99	525	18.86

the sample is very small, that the pattern is more or less the same across the State[10].

Delay Time Distributions

Having examined the gross flows, we now address the second main theme of this chapter, namely the distributions of the lags involved in getting registered or deleted from the Register following coming of age, moving or death. To do this we carried out interviews in the field with respect to about half of the 965 individuals whose names had been identified in the two samples described above. Some 476 interviews were completed, 269 with respect to persons whose names had appeared for the first time on the 1982/83 Register and 207 with respect to persons whose names had been deleted from the 1981/82 Register. These two sets of persons will be referred to as Sample 1 and Sample 2 respectively. Copies of the questionnaire used for these interviews are given in Appendix C.

From the outset it was clear that non-response would be a problem, particularly in the second sample, as many of the people we had identified in the samples were, by definition, geographically mobile. To reduce this difficulty, interviewers were allowed to take information from people other than the named respondents. Since the questions were mainly factual and simple, we did not expect that this would lead to serious inaccuracies, as many

[10]Here and elsewhere we follow the common practice of aggregating the North West and Donegal.

of those contacted by the interviewers could be expected to be relatives of the named respondent or persons living at the contact address. Details of the reasons for non-response were recorded, and in the case of the second sample details of the persons who gave the information about the named respondent were also recorded. These are set out in Table 2.6.

The response rates were better than expected, over 80 per cent in both samples. Two points regarding the figures in the table are worth noting. First, although the response rate in Sample 2 was higher than in Sample 1, the information might be expected to be less complete, since it was usually obtained from a third party. Secondly, the proportion of those who were definitely identified as usually resident at the contact address was 81.1 per cent (including those temporarily away and those too ill to respond). Given that interviews were carried out in November 1982, just over a year after the respondents were recorded as having arrived and as being usually resident, we would have expected to find only about 80 per cent of them still resident on the basis of our findings on chronic mobility described at the end of the previous section. As it turned out, 8.2 per cent of persons could definitely be identified as having left; in other cases the interviewers could obtain no information about the respondent whatsoever and these persons were entered into the 'other' category when Table 2.6 was constructed. We suspect many of the 6.3 per cent of persons in this category were also persons who had recently left. This lends further confirmation to our belief in the existence of a 'chronically' mobile subgroup in the population.

Before proceeding to present the main ideas of this section it is necessary to make one further subdivision of the gross flows described in the previous section. We must use the data from our field survey to divide our estimates of total immigrants into immigrants from abroad and internal migrants. Likewise our estimates of total emigrants will be decomposed into those who went abroad and those who went elsewhere in the State. As in the previous section we rely on the gross flows of names on and off the Register to yield approximations to the corresponding gross flows of persons into and out of the Entitled Electors. Respondents in Sample 1 had been asked to give their previous address and information had been sought about the current address of respondents in Sample 2. Amongst those for whom information was obtained, the breakdown of those identified as having recently moved (excluding persons who were deceased or had just reached the age of franchise) was as given in Table 2.7.

As one might expect, in both samples, the majority of those who were identified as being geographically mobile had made a move within the State. From Table 2.7, the proportion of emigrants who had departed to a destination within the State is found to be 0.9 (98/109) and the proportion of immigrants

Table 2.6: *Details of non-response for both samples together with source of information for the second sample:*

Sample 1 (Response/Non Response)	Number	%
Responded	216	80.3
Respondent too ill to respond	1	0.4
Respondent permanently gone	22	8.2
Respondent temporarily away	1	0.4
Respondent deceased	1	0.4
Information refused	5	1.9
Address could not be located	6	2.2
Other reasons	17	6.3
	269	100.0

Sample 2 (Response/Non Response)	Number	%
Responded (from some party)	180	87.0
No person found to provide information	16	7.7
Information refused	1	0.5
Address could not be located	4	1.9
Other	6	2.9
	207	100.0

Sample 2 (Information Source)	Number	%
Respondent	15	8.3
Relative at above address	59	32.8
Relative at different address	7	3.9
Non-relative at above address	41	22.8
Non-relative at different address	47	26.1
Other	11	6.1
	180	100.0

who had arrived from elsewhere in the State is 0.89 (98/110). Now if the figures given for the total outflow and inflow in Table 2.1 are adjusted for deaths and for those who had reached the age of franchise, respectively, we obtain two statistically independent estimates of the numbers of emigrants and immigrants[11]. When these are multiplied by the estimated proportions of

[11]We have used figures derived from Table 2.1 rather than Table 2.3 as the latter figures would not be independent, but, as we have already remarked, both sets of figures are very similar.

Table 2.7: *Numbers of names in Samples 1 and 2 corresponding to persons who had recently changed address given by origin or destination.*

Origin/Destination	Sample 1 (Old Address)	Sample 2 (New Address)	Total
Within the State	98	98	196
Abroad	12	11	23
Total	110	109	219

emigrants and immigrants which are internal migrants the results are two distinct, independent estimates of the numbers of internal migrants, namely, 144,311 and 159,407. The variances of these estimates may be approximated by a standard formula and hence they may be combined, in proportion to the reciprocals of these variances, to yield an overall estimate of the numbers of internal migrants. This turns out at 153,639. This figure then yields estimates of the flow of emigrants to destinations outside the State and the flow of immigrants from outside the State as residuals to the total emigrant and immigrant figures given in Table 2.3. These are 8,516 (= 162,155 − 153,639) and 22,004 (= 175,643 − 153,639). Table 2.8 summarises all the flows estimated so far.

Table 2.8: *Estimated Outflows from the 1981/82 Register and Inflows to the 1982/83 Register given by type of flow.*

Outflows from the 1981/82 Register		Inflows to the 1982/83 Register	
	'000		'000
Deaths	31.7	Persons reaching age of franchise	66.9
Emigrants abroad	8.5	Immigrants from abroad	22.0
Internal migrants	153.6	Internal migrants	153.6
Total Outflow	193.8	Total Inflow	242.5

The sizes of these flows, considered as approximations to the flow sizes amongst the Entitled Electors, will clearly have a role to play in determining the numbers of errors of the Register. The rapidity with which the Register is adjusted to account for them will also be a determining factor. For example, if these flows are large but the Register is rapidly and accurately updated then the total number of errors of the Register may be quite small. On the other hand, even if the numbers of changes amongst the Entitled Electors were small, the Register could still carry a sizeable number of errors if there are long delays before it is amended to account for them.

In order to establish the pattern of delays in registration (or deletion) we first divided the respondents in Sample 1 into those who had arrived on to the Register as a result of being recently enfranchised and those who had been included as a result of a move. Most of the respondents fell clearly into one of the two categories when reference was made to the questions regarding the time the respondent moved to the contact address and the respondent's age. Amongst the small subgroup of respondents who had both recently come of age and recently moved, we classified all those who were old enough to have been registered at their previous address as immigrants. The remainder were classified as arrivals onto the Register by dint of having reached the age of franchise. In Sample 2 a similar dichotomy was created between those respondents who were deceased and those who had moved away.

Once these four categories (came of age, arrived from elsewhere, deceased, departed to elsewhere) had been created it was possible to examine the distribution of delay times between becoming eligible to be on the Register and actually being registered and between losing eligibility and being removed from it. Thus, a person aged 19 on 15 April 1982 who was found in Sample 1 should have appeared on the 1981/82 Register and, since he did not, we can infer that he had to wait a year to be enfranchised. Likewise a respondent in Sample 2 who had left the contact address prior to 15 September 1978, say, should not have been recorded, at the contact address, on the 1979/80, 1980/81 and 1981/82 Registers. Such an error of the Register would have been outstanding for three years.

A simple model of these delays can be defined as follows. When one of the four above-mentioned events occurs a series of trials ensues. Each trial is constituted by a registration year during which the error created by the event is either corrected (a success) or remains uncorrected (a failure). If the probability of a success remains constant from year to year then it follows that the distribution of delay times between events and their correction is geometric, i.e., the proportion of events occurring in year t-s, say, which are corrected in year t is $g(1-g)^s$ where g is the probability of an error being corrected in a given year. Thus, for example, if the probability of registering a new arrival into the Entitled Electors was 0.7, we would expect 70 per cent of such persons in any year to be listed on the next Register, a further 70 per cent of the remaining 30 per cent, i.e. 21 per cent, would be entered onto the Register one year late, then 70 per cent of the remaining 9 per cent (i.e. 100% - 70% - 21%) would make their appearance on the Register two years after they first became eligible and so on. Note that the number of outstanding errors due to events in a previous year falls very rapidly and so this type of error correction mechanism would satisfy the assumption made at the start of the second section of this chapter.

In order to estimate the parameter g, described above, directly, it would be necessary to obtain a sample of persons who had arrived into or departed from the population of Entitled Electors and to then observe, over a period of years, the times at which the Register was changed to account for these flows. We have at our disposal, however, a sample of persons whose names appeared for the first time or were deleted in a specified year, together with information regarding the time of the events which precipitated these changes of the Register. It will now be shown how these data may be used to obtain an approximate estimate of g for any of the four categories of event.

The reader will recall that we have already established the fact that the flow sizes into and out of the Entitled Electors are changing fairly slowly, the average rates of the period 1971 to 1982 being less than 5 per cent. Thus, to a reasonable approximation, if C_t is the size of any of the four flows in year t we may write:

$$C_t = (1 + r)C_{t-1} = (1 + r)^2 C_{t-2} \ldots = (1 + r)^s C_{t-s},$$
$$\text{or } C_{t-s} = C_t/(1 + r)^s,$$

where r (< 0.05) is the growth rate of the flow size. Now the proportion of events which occurred in year t-s which are corrected in year t is $g(1-g)^s$, thus the number of events from year t-s which are corrected in year t will be:

$$g(1-g)^s C_{t-s} = gh^s C_t/\lambda^s \text{ where } h = 1-g \text{ and } \lambda = 1 + r.$$

The total number of adjustments made in year t as a result of events occurring in all previous years is thus:

$$\sum_{s=0}^{\infty} g\left(\frac{h}{\lambda}\right)^s C_t = g C_t/(1 - h/\lambda)$$
$$= g C_t\lambda/(\lambda - h)$$

So the *proportion* of all adjustments in year t, for any of the four types of event, which is made for events which occurred precisely s years previously is:

$$[g(h/\lambda)^s C_t]/[g C_t\lambda/(\lambda-h)]$$
$$= (h/\lambda)^s (\lambda-h)/\lambda$$
$$= h^s(1 + r - h)/(1 + r)^{s+1}$$

$$= h^s(g + r)/(1 + r)^{s+1} \text{ as } 1 - h = g$$

$$= pq^s$$

where $p = (g + r)/(1 + r)$ and $q = h/(1 + r)$

but as $g + h = 1$, clearly $p + q = 1$, so the distribution of delay times which we may expect to observe in our sample will also be geometric with parameter $p = (g + r)/(1 + r)$. Equivalently, $g = p - (1 - p)r$, and given that r is very small and $(1 - p) < 1$, an estimate of p from the sample will be a good approximation to an estimate of g, so from now on we shall assume $p = g$.

Table 2.9 gives the sample frequency distributions of delay times in each category together with $\hat{p}$, the maximum likelihood estimate of p, the expected frequency distribution given $\hat{p}$ and the value of $1/\hat{p}$, which is the estimated mean delay time in years. Corresponding figures are also given for the cases where the data have been pooled into all arrivals, all departures and all events respectively[12]. The excellent concordance between the actual and expected values in this table indicate that the proposed geometric distribution model is a good fit. Furthermore, it is clear that the distributions of these delay times fade away rapidly as the lag length increases, which confirms the second assumption made at the outset of the chapter. The relative rankings of the correction probabilities, or equivalently, in reverse order, the mean delay times, are as one might expect. Arrivals onto the Register are recorded more quickly than departures, probably because individuals becoming Entitled Electors in an area can draw the Registration authorities attention to their existence, whereas those who have left cannot. Amongst the arrivals, those who have come of age appear to have the lower mean delay time to registration than immigrants; which is probably due to the Registration authority's knowledge of the pre-existing local population. Also deaths are more likely to be reported to the Registration authorities than departures, possibly because there are usually third parties still resident in the same household as the deceased person. Over 70 per cent of all arrivals onto the Register are accounted for on time and this is particularly true of persons reaching the age of franchise where the figure is over 77 per cent. Just short of 60 per cent of all persons who have died or departed have their names removed from the Register in the year in question, deceased persons being slightly more likely to be removed than persons who have moved away.

Estimated Magnitudes of Errors on the Register due to turnover

A person reaching the age of franchise or a death can give rise to one type of error only, the former to a deficiency of the Register, the latter to a surplus. Likewise an immigrant from abroad may fail to be registered or an emigrant to

[12]These pooled estimates are given since they are used at a later stage in chapter 3.

Table 2.9: The distributions of delay times between various categories of events and their correction on the Register given as recorded in the sample and as expected in the sample when a geometric distribution is fitted using the MLE (maximum likelihood estimator) of the parameter p together with p̂ the MLE of p and 1/p̂ the estimated mean of each distribution.

	(1)		(2)		(3)		(4)		(5)		(6)		(7)	
	Came of age		Arrived from elsewhere		Deceased		Departed to elsewhere		All arrivals onto the Register		All departures from the Register		All events	
Delay time (Years)	No.	Expected No.	No.	Expected No.	No.	Expected No.	No.	Expected No.	No.	Expected No.	No.	Expected No.	No.	Expected No.
0 - 1	39	39.4	74	75.1	12	12.5	47	50.0	112	114.4	59	62.4	172	174.4
1 - 2	9	9.0	23	20.9	5	4.7	23	20.9	32	30.0	28	25.7	60	57.8
2 - 3	3	2.0	5	5.8	2	1.8	9	8.8	8	7.8	11	10.6	19	19.1
3 - 4	0	0.5	1	1.6	1	0.7	7	3.7	1	2.0	8	4.3	9	6.3
4 - 5	0	0.1	1	0.4	0	0.2	0	1.5	1	0.5	0	1.8	1	2.0
p̂	0.7727		0.7222		0.625		0.5811		0.7381		0.5889		0.6692	
1/p̂	1.29		1.38		1.6		1.72		1.35		1.70		1.49	

a destination outside the State may incorrectly remain on the Register. A person moving within the State can give rise to one of three different types of error; both at his source and at his destination there are the possibilities of an error arising or an accurate adjustment being made and only accuracy at both places results in no error. Thus, the seven categories of errors due to the turnover of the Register are as follows:

A. Those who have recently reached the age of franchise but who are not yet registered.
B. Deceased persons who have not yet been deleted from the Register.
C. Immigrants from abroad not yet registered.
D. Emigrants to abroad who have not yet been deleted.
E. Internal migrants deleted at their source but not registered at their destination, i.e., persons with no vote.
F. Internal migrants not deleted at their source and registered at their destinations, i.e., persons with two votes.
G. Internal migrants not deleted at their source and not registered at their destination, i.e., persons registered at the wrong place.

Each category of error defines either a group of names which are incorrectly included on the Register or a group of Entitled Electors which have been incorrectly excluded from the Register. Figure 1 shows the relative positions of these categories of error diagramatically.

Figure 2.1: Categories of Error on the Register.

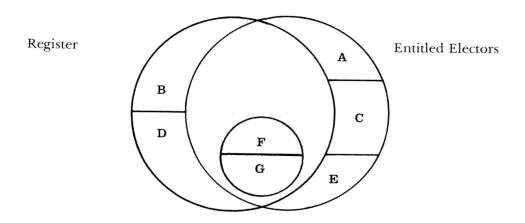

We now consider each of these types of error in turn and provide estimates of their magnitude. These will allow us to assess the overall quality of the Register and the nature of any defects in it. In what follows we shall again invoke our assumptions regarding the approximate constancy of the various flows described above and the reasonably short length of most lags in corrections to the Register. Of course, these assumptions have now been effectively confirmed. As it turns out, our estimates of the numbers of errors in each category are combinations of sums of the form:

$$\sum_{s=0}^{\infty} d^s C_{t-s}$$

where $0 < d < 1$ and C_{t-s} is the size of one of the flows described in Table 2.8 in the year s years prior to the current year, t. In other words, the sizes of the error categories will be shown to be made up of weighted sums of the sizes of certain flows over past years. Such sums will always be approximated as:

$$\sum_{s=0}^{\infty} d^s C_t = [1/(1-d)]C_t$$

where C_t is the flow size over the current year t, which for our purposes is 1982. The approximation is justified in the same way as that made in equation (2.2) of the second section of this chapter. Indeed a partial summation over the first few terms of this series would provide a perfectly adequate approximation to the complete sum. However, as the reader shall see, the infinite sums in question are easy to compute and have a natural interpretation.

Category A: Those persons who have reached the age of franchise but who are not yet registered: Consider the proportion of people who reached the age of franchise in year t-s who have still not been registered by year t. For s = 0 it is just (1-p), where p (0.7727 derived from column 1 of Table 2.9) is the probability that an 18 year old is registered during the year he becomes eligible to vote. For s = 1 the proportion is $(1-p)^2$, that is, the proportion of 19 year olds (persons who were 18 years old one year previously) who have failed to be registered for two years in succession. In general this proportion is $(1-p)^{s+1}$, thus adding up the numbers of persons from each different previous years who have still not registered we obtain:

$$\sum_{s=0}^{\infty} (1-p)^{s+1} C_{t-s}$$

where in this case C_{t-s} is the number of persons who became 18 years of age s years prior to the current year. As explained above this may be approximated by:

$$\sum_{s=0}^{\infty} (1-p)^{s+1} C_t = mC_t$$

where $m = \dfrac{(1-p)}{1-(1-p)} = \dfrac{1-p}{p}$

When the *multiplier*, m, is calculated with the value of p = 0.7727, we get m = 0.2942. Now taking C_t to be the size of a cohort of 18 year olds as given in Table 2.8 the total number of errors in category A is estimated as:

$$mC_t = 0.2942 \times 66,900 = 19,700$$

Note. that m = (1/p).q where q = (1-p) is the probability of an error arising. Since 1/p is the mean delay time, the value of mC_t may be interpreted as the number of persons in the flow C_t who cause some error, qC_t, multiplied by the average length of time for which an error is outstanding.

Category B: Deceased persons who have been deleted: This category may be dealt with in exactly the same way as Category A. Here, the appropriate value of the correction probability, p, is 0.625 (derived from column 2 of Table 2.9) and hence the corresponding value of the multiplier, m, is m = (1-0.625)/0.625 = 0.6. Using the figure of 31,700 given in Table 2.8 for the number of deaths amongst those over 18 years, our estimate for the number of errors in this category is 0.6 × 31,700 = 19,000.

Category C: Immigrants from abroad not yet registered: Again the method used to obtain an estimate for this category is the same as for the preceding two categories. The appropriate value of p is 0.7222 and the multiplier is 0.3847. As the size of the flow of immigrants was estimated to be 22,000 at the start of this section, the estimate for the number of errors in Category C is 0.3847 × 22,000 = 8,500. Admittedly it may not be particularly realistic in this case to assume that the sizes of the flows of immigrants are approximately constant. However, as the reader shall see, the number of errors in this category must be very small in comparison to those in the other error categories, and even if our figure is a relatively poor estimate, it can only have a marginal effect on our overall results.

Category D: Emigrants abroad who have not been deleted: Here p = 0.5811, the multiplier is 0.7209 and the estimate for the numbers in this category is 0.7209 × 8,500 = 6,100. As with Categories A, B and C this figure may be interpreted as the number of errors created by a flow multiplied by the average amount of time for which these errors are outstanding. Again, even if the flow sizes vary somewhat from year to year this should not greatly affect our overall results.

Category E: Internal migrants deleted at their source but not registered at their destination, i.e., persons with no vote: This is the first of the three categories of error where both inclusion and deletion probabilities must be considered. For present purposes let p be the probability that an arrival is registered when it occurs (0.7222), let a be the probability that a departing person's name is removed from the Register on time (0.5811) and let q = 1-p and b = 1-a. It is not unreasonable to assume that the two events, deletion at source and inclusion at destination, are independent. The proportion of the group of individuals who moved s years ago and who have not been deleted at their source is $(1\text{-}a)^{s+1} = b^{s+1}$, which may be derived in the same way as the corresponding expressions for Categories B and D. Thus the proportion of this group who have been deleted at their source is $1 - b^{s+1}$. Now the proportion of those who moved s years ago who have not been included at their destination is $(1\text{-}p)^{s+1} = q^{s+1}$, hence the proportion who have been deleted but have not been included is:

$$v_s = q^{s+1}(1 - b^{s+1})$$

Summing over all previous years gives the multplier:

$$m = \sum_{s=0}^{\infty} v_s = \sum_{s=0}^{\infty} [q^{s+1} - (qb)^{s+1}]$$

$$= \frac{q}{1-q} - \frac{qb}{1-qb} = 0.2530$$

which, when applied to our earlier estimate of the flow of internal migrants in any one year of 153,600, yields 38,900 as our estimate of the numbers of persons in this category. The interpretation of the formula for the multiplier given here is more subtle. The term $qC_t/(1\text{-}q)$ is the total number of internal migrants who have not been registered at their destinations. However, as we are exclusively concerned with errors of this type which are created by persons whose names have not been erroneously retained on the Register at their source, we must subtract from this figure the number of persons who create both types of error. But the probability of creating both errors is qb, thus, as we might expect from our earlier analyses, the correct term to subtract is:
$qbC_t/(1\text{-}qb)$, as above.

Category F: Internal migrants not deleted at their source and registered at their destinations, i.e., persons with two votes: Here we have a mirror image of category E. The two things that happen to migrants in category E do not happen to persons in category F. Thus the appropriate series to sum to obtain the multiplier is:

$$\sum_{s=0}^{\infty} b^{s+1}(1-q^{s+1}) = \frac{b}{1-b} - \frac{qb}{1-qb} = 0.5892$$

Grossing gives $0.5892 \times 153,600 = 90,500$ as our estimate of the number of persons with two votes. An interpretation of the multiplier similar to that given for category E applies to this category.

Category G: Internal migrants not deleted at their source and not registered at their destination, i.e., persons with a vote at the wrong place. From our remarks concerning category E we already know the multiplier for this category. For completeness we present it as the sum of the appropriate series:

$$m = \sum_{s=0}^{\infty} b^{s+1} q^{s+1} = qb/(1-qb) = 0.1317$$

yielding an estimate of 20,200 persons with a vote at their old address, not at their current address.

The estimates presented above were made using sample estimates of the various correction probabilities involved. As such the multipliers used and hence the estimates are naturally subject to sampling variation, so we attempted to obtain some idea of the degree to which this could affect them. Our estimate of any given correction probability, $\hat{p}$ say, is the ratio of a fixed number of successes, S, namely, a number of names identified as having arrived into or having been deleted from the Register, to a number of trials T, being the total number of years waited amongst all respondents for an appropriate correction to be made in their cases. It is well known, see Kendall and Stuart, (1967), that in these circumstances $\hat{p}$ is approximately distributed as:

$$\hat{p} \sim N(p, p^2(1-p)/T)$$

where p is the parameter being estimated. Thus the variance of this distribution may be estimated using $\hat{p}$ itself as $\hat{p}^2(1-\hat{p})/T$. In order to obtain approximations to the sampling distributions of the multipliers the following simulations were carried out. For each multiplier formula:

(i) 10,000 random values of $\hat{p}$ and/or $\hat{a}$ as appropriate were generated using the approximation to their distributions described above;
(ii) The multiplier formula was calculated;

(iii) The resulting value was tabulated.

From the frequency tables built up in this way it was possible to create 90 per cent confidence intervals for the values of the multiplier, which, when applied to the appropriate flow sizes, gave approximate confidence intervals for the sizes of the error categories. Of course the flow sizes which we estimated from the sample are themselves random variables and this will also contribute to the variances of our estimates. But their effect in this connection is relatively small when compared with the effect of the sampling distributions of the parameters and so we have omitted it from our calculations of the confidence intervals[13].

All the preceding estimates, together with their corresponding confidence intervals are assembled in Table 2.10. This gives an overall picture of the errors of the Register and their sources, excluding, of course, the Dublin Stockpile which will be dealt with presently[14]. The surplus of names on the 1982/83 Register due to turnover is made up of those in categories B, D and F and stands at 115,600. Deficiencies, which are caused by categories A, C and E amount to 67,100 Entitled Electors. This gives a gross error due to turnover of 182,700 and a net error of 48,500, the latter being the difference between the surplus and the deficiency. We also obtain from these figures an estimate of the numbers of Entitled Electors. All that is necessary is to subtract the surplus and add the deficiency to the Register and the result should be the number of persons which the Register would contain if there were no errors due to turnover. When this is done we obtain a figure of 2,261,800 or 97.9 per cent of the adjusted 1982/83 Register. Note that if, as we have suggested, the error structure of the Register is relatively stable, then an equivalent figure for the Entitled Electors in 1981 is given by this percentage of the adjusted 1981/82 Register, i.e., 2,214,300.

The estimate of the numbers of Entitled Electors which is implied by our

[13]The flows for categories A and B are non-stochastic as they are taken from census data, hence they are not a problem. Extremely conservative confidence intervals for the important categories E, F and G may be constructed by using the confidence intervals for the gross flows given in Table 2.2. At worst this would amount to changing the bounds by less than 15 per cent.

[14]As explained in the text these estimates were made on the assumption that the growth rate of any flow is zero. It is, however, possible to develop formulae for the multipliers when these growth rates are non zero. Simultaneously it is also necessary to allow for the fact that the estimated correction probabilities are not the true correction probabilities (see text). Fortunately these two effects tend to cancel each other out. For example, if there is positive growth in the flows then using the current value of the flow as an approximation to all previous values tends to over estimate the size of the error category. But in that case we have also over estimated the true correction probability which has the effect of understating the numbers of errors. Thus when the multipliers were calculated using annual growth rates between -5 per cent and +5 per cent the error estimates were only slightly affected.

Table 2.10: The multipliers for each category of error, together with the relevant flow sizes, the estimates of the numbers in each category and the 90 per cent confidence intervals for the Registration year 1982/83.

Category	Multiplier	Flow Size	Estimated Errors for the Category	90% Confidence Interval Lower Bound	Upper Bound
		'000	'000	'000	'000
A (Came of Age)	0.2942	66.9	19.7	11.0	31.2
B (Deceased)	0.6	31.7	19.0	9.6	31.8
C (Immigrants)	0.3847	22.0	8.5	6.1	11.3
D (Emigrants)	0.7209	8.5	6.1	4.6	8.0
E (No Vote)	0.2530	153.6	38.9	26.7	55.9
F (Double Registration)	0.5892	153.6	90.5	66.5	123.3
G (Vote at Wrong Place)	0.1317	153.6	20.2	14.3	27.1
H Surplus (B + D + F)	—	—	115.6	80.7*	163.1*
I Deficiency (A + C + E)	—	—	67.1	43.8*	98.4*

*These confidence intervals are conservative as they can only be achieved if each of their components is realised, i.e., each category is equal to its lower (respectively upper) confidence bound.

estimates of the numbers of persons in each of the error categories may be cross-checked by reference to census data since, by definition, the Entitled Electors are persons aged 18 years and over who are resident in the State. A problem arises here because of the *de facto* nature of the census and the date of the census. The Register exists as a variable only in discrete time; for an entire registration year it refers to those who were usually resident at a given location at a given point in time. Thus, for example, a person who was resident at location A in, say, September 1978 and moved to location B in January 1979 would not cause an error of the Register for the registration year 1979/80.

Only if he failed to be registered at location B for the 1980/81 year, given that he was still resident there in September 1980, would his move create an error. The population, however, is a continuously changing variable which is measured by the Census at a particular point in time, April of the Census year. For this reason the difference between the Census figure for persons aged 18 years and over in April and the Register, which refers to the previous September, will be made up of genuine errors of the Register as compiled in September and discrepancies which are the result of changes in the intervening 6.5 months. This difference, between the population aged 18 years and over and the Register, will reach a peak the following September at which point a new Register will be prepared and, if our model is correct, about 60 per cent to 70 per cent of the outstanding differences will be corrected. The residual of this process becomes the new set of errors of the new Register. Thus, before comparing our estimate of the numbers of Entitled Electors for the 1981/82 Registration year with the numbers of persons aged 18 years and over reported in the 1981 Census, some allowance must be made for events which occurred between September 1980 and April 1981.

As we only intend to compare figures for the State as a whole internal migration between September and April will not cause a problem. An internal migrant will be counted once and only once at Census time regardless of his location. As net external migration was relatively low at that time (annual net migration between 1979 and 1981 was -4,380 persons) the main adjustment necessary is for deaths[15]. Using the Quarterly Reports on Births, Marriages and Deaths, a figure of 18,000 deaths amongst persons aged 18 years and over was calculated to have occurred between September 1980 and April 1981. Volume II of the 1981 Census reports a figure of 2,197,000 persons as being aged 18 years and over in April 1981, hence the number of Entitled Electors who should have appeared on the 1981/82 Register is 2,215,000, since people who

---

[15]With respect to external migration the inflow and outflow will cancel, thus the net flow is the figure which is relevant for these adjustments. If the annual flow is spread evenly across the year the flow in the 6.5 months between Septemberr and April will be in the order of 2,400 persons and this includes all persons both over *and* under 18 years of age. In other words the effect of external net migration should be very small.

died between September and April should, nevertheless, have been registered. This figure compares very favourably with the number implied by our error estimates of 2,214,300, given above.

The good agreement between the figures would suggest that the categories of error which we have defined are nearly exhaustive. In particular, errors that arise from turnover on the Register would appear to account for nearly all the errors of the Register and that if errors arise in some other way they are negligible. For example, there may be groups of persons who never become enfranchised: those who reach the age of franchise but die before being admitted onto the Register would be such a group. Also, the figures used in creating these estimates have already been changed to account for the Dublin stockpile, which grew quite rapidly over the period 1981-1982, so the concordance between the two figures suggests that our adjustments for this phenomenon are reasonably accurate.

It is interesting to compare our results with a similar study of the Electoral Register in the United Kingdom (Todd and Butcher, 1982). Again the results excluding the Dublin stockpile are appropriate since this is an isolated phenomenon. Their figure for total surplus or redundant names was between 6.1 per cent and 9.4 per cent. The corresponding figure from our study was 5.0 per cent. Their estimate of the deficiency was also higher than ours, 6.5 per cent as against 3.0 per cent. It must be borne in mind that, unlike our approach, the British study was based on a comparison of the Register with the Census. Hence, persons whose names never appear on the Register would be identified whereas they would be overlooked in our study. However we have good reason to believe that there are very few people in this group in Ireland. Most of the difference is probably caused by the higher rate of internal mobility in Britain. Devis (1983) shows that as many as 9.6 per cent of the population of Great Britain changed their address in the year 1980-81. This implies an even higher mobility rate amongst those aged 18 years and over. The overall rate appears substantially in excess of the corresponding rate for Ireland which was 6.1 per cent in 1981 and which is unlikely to have changed greatly over one year in view of our comparisons in the first section of this chapter.

The Dublin Stockpile

We now introduce an explicit analysis of the stockpile of names which gives the Dublin Register its special nature. Our adjustments to this Register (see Appendix A) begin in 1979. The implied sizes of the stockpile and the corresponding flows into the stockpile are given below for the years 1979 to 1982. As explained in the Appendix these flows onto the stockpile are the result of people leaving and not being deleted. If we may assume they are re-

registered elsewhere according to our scheme of inclusion probabilities we may estimate the extra numbers of persons in each of the relevant categories (D, F and G). To be thorough we have divided these outflows of people into external migrants and internal migrants.

Table 2.11: *Details of the Dublin stockpile of names and the flows onto it for the years 1979 to 1982.*

	Total Stockpile	Flow into Stockpile	=	Emigrants* to abroad	+	Internal Migrants*
1979	4,485	4,485		307		4,178
1980	18,073	13,588		931		12,657
1981	31,661	13,588		931		12,657
1982	45,249	13,588		931		12,657

*(The division of the total flow into emigrants and internal migrants was made using the percentage of all persons in Sample 2 who were recorded as emigrants).

Among the internal migrants whose names remain on the stockpile we can calculate the number who will by now be registered elsewhere. A total of 37,359 are estimated to be in this category (F). All of the estimated 3,100 emigrants must be assigned to category D since the question of their re-registration is irrelevant. The remaining 4,790 may be ascribed to category G, i.e., persons with a vote at the wrong place.

It is possible to give an indication of the geographical location of the stockpile within Dublin Borough. The Borough is divided into 141 wards (district electoral divisions) for which data from the census and from the Register are available. For each of these areas we computed the value R_{82}/C_{81} where R_{82} is the numbers on the 1982/83 Register (which refers to those usually resident in September 1981) and C_{81} is the population as reported in the 1981 Census. Generally this figure could be expected to range about 0.7 which was the ratio of the numbers of persons 18 years of age and over to the total population for the borough as a whole in 1981. We presumed that for wards where the stockpile was concentrated a much higher value of this ratio would be observed, in particular a ranking of these values should identify the location of the stockpile. Choosing 0.85 as an arbitrary cut off point we found that for 32 wards the ratio R_{82}/C_{81} was in excess of this value. These wards are depicted in Figure 2 which gives their position on a map of the borough area. As can be seen from this map the stockpile is concentrated in two belts: one belt north of the city centre: and one south of the Grand Canal. This is not surprising since

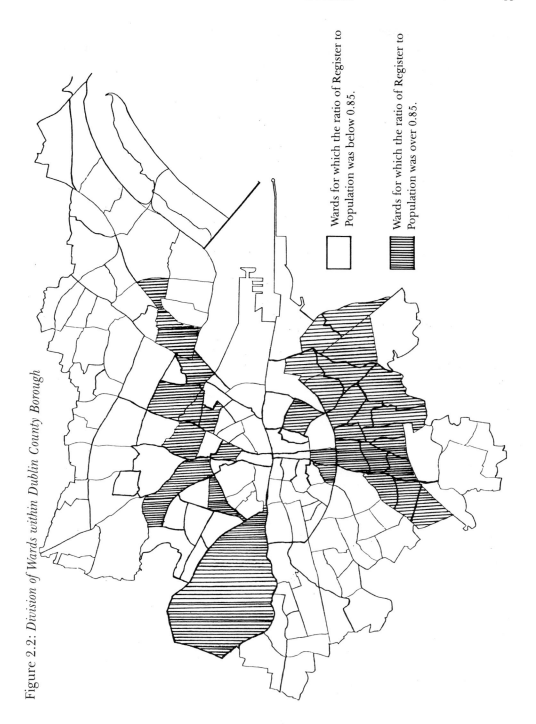

Figure 2.2: *Division of Wards within Dublin County Borough*

Wards for which the ratio of Register to Population was below 0.85.

Wards for which the ratio of Register to Population was over 0.85.

these areas are characterized by high proportions of their populations living in short-term rented accommodation and are presumably the location of a large number of those who are chronically mobile. These are, in turn, precisely the individuals who can be expected to create the stockpile if it is formed in the way we have hypothesised.

The total population of these 32 wards in 1981 was 101,634 and the corresponding figure for the Register was 97,004. Using the ratio of 0.7 described above these areas may be expected to have contained about 71,000 persons of 18 years and over, giving a surplus for the register of about 27,000. Some of this surplus can be explained in terms of natural turnover errors. However, given our figures for the State as a whole, this is unlikely to account for more than a few thousand names. As our estimate of the stockpile of 1981 was 31,661 these areas would seem to account for most of it.

There is some evidence that the stockpile is now lower than its peak level of 1982: the 1983/84 and 1984/85 Register stood at 377,122 and 384,512 respectively, a fall from the 1982/83 level of 392,765. Nevertheless these values are still substantially in excess of the 366,489 persons of 18 years and over which are reported to have been present in the borough in 1981, and the borough population is falling!

Table 2.12. *Estimates of the errors of the 1982/83 Register in various categories showing the breakdown into errors arising through turnover and those due to the stockpile in Dublin.*

Category	(1) Turnover Errors	(2) Dublin Stockpile	(3) = (1) + (2) Total
	'000	'000	'000
A (Came of Age)	19.7	—	19.7
B (Deaths)	19.0	—	19.0
C (Immigrants)	8.5	—	8.5
D (Emigrants)	6.1	3.1	9.2
E (No Vote)	38.9	—	38.9
F (Double Registration)	90.5	37.4	127.9
G (Wrong Place)	20.2	4.8	25.0
H Surplus (B + D + F)	115.6	40.5	156.1
I Deficiency (A + C + E)	67.1	0	67.1
J Gross Error (H + I)	182.7	40.5	223.2
K Net Error (H − I)	48.5	40.5	89.0
L Implied Entitled Electors	—	—	2,221.3

Table 2.12 gives the breakdown of all errors of the Register in 1982 including those due to the stockpile. These estimates will form the basis of our discussion in the following chapters which consider in turn the implications for population estimation, sample selection and the electoral system. For the present, therefore, we will confine our comments to a description of the overall patterns and postpone discussion of implications until later.

The gross total number of errors is over 220,000 or about 9.5 per cent of the Register. This is compared to a surplus of about 156,000, names which are on the Register but should not be, and a deficiency of 67,000 persons who should have a vote but do not. There are, in addition, some 28,000 persons who are registered in the wrong place, i.e., at their former address. About a quarter of the overall surplus, one-fifth of the gross errors, is attributable to the Dublin stockpile effect. The most frequent single item of error is double registration which accounts for over half of the errors.

Socio demographic characteristics of movers

The final section of this chapter attempts to give information on the kinds of people who create the errors due to turnover of the Register. The likely socio-demographic characteristics of young persons who have not yet been enfranchised, almost entirely 18 to 20 year olds, and persons who are recently deceased are clear. We concentrate therefore on describing these characteristics for migrants.

Our survey obtained data on the sex, age, marital status, nationality and occupation of each respondent. When the results for these variables were tabulated it was clear there were no systematic differences between Samples 1 and 2 in these respects. As noted earlier the vast majority of the respondents were internal migrants and hence the two samples were effectively samples of the same population. Accordingly the results of the two samples were pooled. Details of the breakdown are given in Table 2.13 below. This table also gives the corresponding percentage breakdown in the various categories for persons aged 20 years and over, who were found to have a different address from one year previously in the 1971 census, and for all persons aged 20 years and over in the 1979 census.

For the categories analysed in the table there is evidence that the socio-demographic characteristics of those who move show the same pattern found in most developed countries, see Shaw (1975). The propensity to migrate varies inversely with age. Generally the propensity to migrate is not particularly selective with respect to sex and those of professional and managerial occupations are more migratory than their counterparts. We tested these hypotheses formally using the usual X^2 test to compare the distri-

Table 2.18: *Breakdown of movers identified in the sample into selected socio demographic classifications given in gross and as percentages together with the corresponding percentages amongst movers in the 1971 census and for the population as a whole. This table also includes the chi-square goodness of fit statistics for the sample distributions compared with the 1971 Census (movers) and 1979 Census distributions respectively.*

		Sample Number	Sample %	Census 1971 (movers) %	Census 1979 %	X^2 (1971)	X^2 (1979)	X^2 degrees of freedom
Sex	Male	111	48.7	47.13	49.7	0.22	0.09	1
	Female	117	51.3	52.87	50.3			
Age	20 - 24	53	23.2	31.25	13.2			
	25 - 29	66	28.9	24.45	11.8			
	30 - 39	42	18.4	20.00	19.7			
	40 - 49	29	12.7	8.65	15.4			
	50 - 59	19	8.3	5.55	15.1			
	60 +	19	8.3	10.09	24.7	15.09	107.14	5
Marital Status	Single	71	28.7	31.57	29.7			
	Married	166	67.2	64.10	61.9	1.04	7.54	2
	Widowed	10	4.0	4.32	8.8			
Nationality	Irish	237	95.2	n.a.	n.a.	—	—	—
	Other	12	4.8	n.a.	n.a.			
Occupation	Agricultural workers	9	3.9(5.5)*	5.29+	20.5**			
	Producers, makers and repairers	39	16.8(23.6)	18.76	21.3			
	Labourers and unskilled workers	8	3.4(4.8)	5.44	5.4			
	Transport and communication workers	10	4.3(6.1)	6.65	7.0			
	Clerical workers	15	6.5(9.1)	15.76	10.3			
	Commerce, insurance and finance workers	26	11.2(15.8)	9.62	10.1			
	Service workers	17	7.3(10.3)	12.24	7.1			
	Professional and technical workers	41	17.7(24.8)	26.25	18.3	14.04	30.66	7
	Housewife	63	27.2	—	—			
	Student	4	1.7	—	—			

* Percentages when housewives and students are excluded.

** Corresponding percentages from the 1979 Labour Force Survey.

+ Gainfully occupied persons aged 14 years and over.

butions based on the sample with those given for movers from the 1971 census and for all persons from the 1979 census[16]. As expected our sample of migrants reflected the results of the 1971 census with respect to movers[17]. The only occasion for which there was a significant difference at the 5 per cent level was in respect of age. But it should be remembered that the non-respondents in our survey were primarily chronic movers, who in turn are concentrated amongst the young. Thus they are likely to be somewhat under represented. Although the X^2 statistic for the comparison of the occupational distributions is, admittedly, large, it is not actually significant. In any case, as it was only possible to compare the distribution of gainfully employed persons aged 14 years and over who had moved in 1971 with persons aged 20 years and over from the sample, some discrepancy was to be expected. In particular the relative sizes of the Clerical, as opposed to Commerce, Insurance and Finance categories will be different. This comparison was made excluding housewives and students. When the sample percentages were compared with the corresponding percentages for the population as a whole, the pattern of significant differences confirmed our remarks about the socio-demographic characteristics of movers given above the X^2 statistics were significant for age and occupation but not for the other categories.

Finally we examine the answers given regarding the reason for respondents' moves. Table 2.14 shows that nearly half of those who moved did so for reasons of needing a different dwelling. If categories 2, 3 and 4 of this table are combined it is seen that about 20 per cent of persons moved for job related reasons. When the categories of reasons for moving are collapsed into job-related reasons and non-job-related reasons a clear pattern emerges. Table 2.15 shows that over 90 per cent of within county movements are not job-related whereas over 40 per cent of movements across county boundaries are job-related. The reader may also note that within county movements account for 58 per cent of all movements, a figure which compares reasonably well with that of 53 per cent recorded in the 1981 census.

Conclusions

In this chapter we have shown that the gross turnovers of the Register constitute fairly stable proportions of the Register and for this reason they may be used as approximations to the gross turnovers of the population of Entitled Electors. The outflow is in the region of 8.5 per cent of the Register's size, the inflow is about 10.5 per cent. We have also shown that the distributions of delay

[16]For the occupational breakdown, the percentages from the 1979 Labour Force Survey were used.

[17]A detailed analysis of internal migration in Ireland is given in Hughes and Walsh (1980).

Table 2.14: *Reasons given for moving.*

	Reasons for Moving	Number	%
1.	Built or needed a new dwelling	107	45.9
2.	Went to a new job (new employer)	27	11.5
3.	Went to look for a job	8	3.4
4.	Business/Work reasons (same employer)	14	6.0
5.	Moved out of house/home	2	0.9
6.	Educational reasons	2	0.9
7.	Got married	39	16.7
8.	Retired	8	3.4
9.	Other reasons	26	11.3
		233	100.0

Table 2.15: *Employment and non-employment related reasons for moving, cross classified by whether the movement was within county or external.*

	Same County		Other County/Abroad	
	Persons	(%)	Persons	(%)
Employment Related	10	(8.1)	37	(41.6)
Non-employment Related	113	(91.9)	52	(58.4)
	123	(100.0)	89	(100.0)

times between events in the population of Entitled Electors and their subsequent recordings on the Register are geometric. About 60 per cent of all outflows are recorded within one year, i.e., when the next Register is prepared, and just over 70 per cent of all inflows are inserted into the Register in the same period.

Gross errors account for about 9.5 per cent of the total Register. These gross errors are composed of a surplus of about 156,000 names (6 per cent) and a deficiency of some 67,000 persons (3 per cent), the most common problem being double registration. The stockpile in Dublin accounted for about a fifth of all errors of the 1982/83 Register. The model used to make these estimates predicts a net error, i.e., the surplus minus the deficiency, of about 89,000 persons, or 49,000 persons when the Dublin stockpile is excluded. This compares favourably with an alternative estimate of the net error which may be made by reference to census data. We also found that the socio-demographic characteristics of migrants, who are the primary sources of the flows, and hence the errors of the Register, are similar to those of migrants in other developed countries. In general the composition of these flows of persons appear to have changed little since 1971.

The fact that the structure of the Register's dynamics appears to be historically stable would seem to constitute reasonable grounds for modelling the number of names on each county's Register as stationary stochastic processes. This is done in chapter 3. Using the results of chapter 3, models for generating population estimates are developed in chapter 4. Chapter 5 considers how random samples may be selected from the Register. All three chapters rely heavily on the present chapter.

Chapter 3

THE DYNAMICS OF THE REGISTER

Introduction

The primary purposes of this chapter are technical ones. First, we know that the flows into and out of the Register lag behind those of the population of Entitled Electors. We previously showed the approximate equalities of some of these flows over short periods of time, and that it was appropriate for us to make the working hypothesis that they were equal when we made our estimates of the errors of the Register, presented in the last chapter. However, when we come to study the Register as a time series over a relatively long period of time it is necessary to take the differences between the flows into account. We only have data on the Register, the numbers of Entitled Electors cannot be directly observed. Nevertheless, using the results of chapter 2, we are able to show that a suitable transformation of the net flows of the Register should be a good approximation to the net flows of Entitled Electors and in this way we can build up an approximate Entitled Elector series. This is discussed in the second section of this chapter. Secondly, even the population of Entitled Electors contains a certain random element which we must try to remove if we wish to use these data for population estimation, i.e., as an independent variable in a regression model with the census population figures as a dependent variable. In particular we seek to remove the 'noisy' component of this population, which is made up of highly mobile people and whose relationship to the census population (at census time) must be very slight. The removal of this component from the series also helps to mitigate a problem considered in the penultimate section of Whelan and Keogh (1980). In that paper it was pointed out that the migration series presented, which was derived from a sequence of population estimates based on the Register, was highly variable, and that a moving average of these population estimates might be used to reduce the problem. We now feel that the best remedy is to tackle the stochastic element of this series at its source, namely, to remove the noisy component of the series on which our new population estimates shall be based. This is done in the third section of the chapter. In the fourth section we present a simplified method of implementing the analyses in the earlier sections to produce the estimates of the numbers of Entitled Electors previously discussed, and this method may also be used to produce future estimates of this series as fresh Registers appear.

The Relationship between the Register and Entitled Electors

Using the notation of the previous chapter the Register in year t will be denoted R_t. The corresponding inflows and outflows of the Register will be denoted F_t and G_t respectively. The Entitled Electors in year t will be denoted E_t and its flows, inflow and outflow respectively, by X_t and Y_t. Thus:

$$R_{t+1} = R_t + F_t - G_t \tag{3.1}$$

$$E_{t+1} = E_t + X_t - Y_t \tag{3.2}$$

Note that this implies equality between first differences and net flows.

$$\Delta R_{t+1} = R_{t+1} - R_t = F_t - G_t$$

$$\Delta E_{t+1} = E_{t+1} - E_t = X_t - Y_t$$

Although we do not have direct observations on E_t, we do know the approximate form of the relationship between the flows into and out of E_t and those into and out of R_t. From Chapter 2 equation (2.2):

$$F_t = pX_t + pqX_{t-1} + pq^2X_{t-2} + \ldots \tag{3.3}$$

where p is the probability of being included on the Register in the year an individual becomes eligible and $q = 1-p$[18]. Likewise:

$$G_t = aY_t + abY_{t-1} + ab^2Y_{t-2} + \ldots \tag{3.4}$$

where a is the deletion probability and $b = 1-a$. These probabilities may change over time. However, given the registration authorities' overall agreement that the system has changed little since 1960 and our observations concerning the apparent stability of the whole process we shall use the sample estimates. We believe that to whatever extent these probabilities deviated from our current estimates in the past, this is still a better option than assuming they are unity!

From equation 3.3 we have:

$$qF_{t-1} = pqX_{t-1} + pq^2X_{t-2} + pq^3X_{t-3} + \ldots \tag{3.5}$$

---

[18] For simplicity we assume that the difference between the values of p for persons reaching age of franchise and for immigrants may be ignored. The same assumption is used with respect to the difference between the correction probabilities for deaths and for emigrants. It becomes clear from the argument that follows that a more elaborate version of that argument would establish the validity of these assumptions.

Hence, subtracting (3.5) from (3.3):

$$F_t - qF_{t-1} = pX_t$$

Likewise:

$$G_t - bG_{t-1} = aY_t$$

Now as $a < p$ (see Table 2.9) for any Θ with $a < \Theta < p$ we may write:

$$p = \Theta + \delta_1, a = \Theta - \delta_2$$

so: $q = 1 - (\Theta + \delta_1)$ and $b = 1 - (\Theta - \delta_2)$

which gives:

$$F_t - (1 - \Theta - \delta_1)F_{t-1} = (\Theta + \delta_1)X_t \qquad (3.6)$$
$$G_t - (1 - \Theta + \delta_2)G_{t-1} = (\Theta - \delta_2)Y_t \qquad (3.7)$$

Subtracting (3.7) from (3.6) yields:

$$(F_t - G_t) - (1 - \Theta)(F_{t-1} - G_{t-1}) + \delta_1 F_{t-1} + \delta_2 G_{t-1}$$
$$= \Theta(X_t - Y_t) + \delta_1 X_t + \delta_2 Y_t$$

As $F_t - G_t = \Delta R_t$ and $X_t - Y_t = \Delta E_t$, we have:

$$\Delta R_t - (1 - \Theta)\Delta R_{t-1} = \Theta \Delta E_t + \delta_1(X_t - F_{t-1}) + \delta_2(Y_t - G_{t-1})$$

or

$$\Delta E_t = \frac{1}{\Theta}(\Delta R_t - (1 - \Theta)\Delta R_{t-1}) - \frac{\delta_1}{\Theta}(X_t - F_{t-1}) - \frac{\delta_2}{\Theta}(Y_t - G_{t-1})$$
$$(3.8)$$

This equation gives the net flows of Entitled Electors in terms of the net flows of the Register and differences between their respective gross inflows and outflows. Of course, only the first term on the right hand side of (3.8) can be calculated from the time series data on the Register, after a suitable value of Θ, lying between the inflow and outflow correction probabilities, has been chosen. The extent to which this term is a valid approximation to ΔE_t will thus depend on the values of the final two terms. If $a = p$ then $\delta_1 = \delta_2 = 0$ and the approximation is exact. For small values of δ_1 and δ_2 it should still be reasonably good, particularly as each of the final terms is made up of the difference of two values which are of the same order of magnitude ($X_t \doteqdot F_{t-1}$ and $Y_t \doteqdot G_{t-1}$) and these are themselves multiplied by relatively small numbers

$(\delta_1/\Theta$ and $\delta_2/\Theta)$. In other words we have an approximation to E_t as:

$$\Delta E_t \doteq \frac{1}{\Theta}(\Delta R_t - (1 - \Delta)\Theta R_{t-1})$$

We choose $\Theta = 0.6692$, which is the value of the parameter estimated from the geometric distribution model when all delay times are pooled (see Table 2.9). If we ignore the small differences between the estimated inclusion probabilities for births and immigrants and between the deletion probabilities for deaths and emigrants then the (pooled) estimates for p and a are 0.7381 and 0.5889 respectively. Thus the values of δ_1 and δ_2 are $\delta_1 = 0.7381 - 0.6692 = 0.0689$ and $\delta_2 = 0.6692 - 0.5889 = 0.0803$. In effect then, we have argued that the assumption that $a = \Theta = p$ should not seriously distort our approximation to ΔE_r[19]. Accordingly, using the adjusted data on the Register for the years 1955 to 1982, we were able to form a series for the net flows of Entitled Electors for the years ending in 1957 to 1982 for each county[20].

The stochastic properties of E_t

Our next task was to attempt to purge at least some of the purely random component from the derived series of flows of Entitled Electors. As we had only 26 observations on these series for each county we did not have a great deal of scope to fit particularly elaborate models, but as it turned out, a relatively simple model fitted these data quite well. Following the standard approach we differenced the variable $Z_t = \Delta E_t$ until the vaiance of the resulting variable was at a minimum. For each county this occurred after one round of differencing, thus the variable to which we fitted our model was $Z_t = \Delta^2 E_t$. Given the very short length of these time series we decided on a simple autoregressive model of degree 1, i.e.,:

$$\Delta Z_t = c + p\Delta Z_{t-1} + \epsilon_t \dots (3.9)$$

where c and p are parameters and ϵ_t is a random disturbance. At the outset there were two aspects of this model that we wished to examine.
(i) Whether the value of p lay between -1 and 1, a necessary and sufficient condition for the process to be stationary.
(ii) Whether the constant c was significantly different from zero.

The model was estimated for each of the thirty-one regions using ordinary least squares. After the single differencing and due to the fact that the model

[19]Note that the fact that $a \neq p$ was of crucial importance in chapter 2, where we were attempting to estimate figures associated with gross flows.

[20]See Appendix A for a discussion of the need to adjust the data and the procedures used.

involved a lagged regressor there were 24 observations available. Details of the results are given in Table 3.1

With regard to (i) above the results were satisfactory, each estimated value of ρ lay between -1 and 1. All but three of the values of ρ were significantly different from 0 at the 5 per cent level, although it should be remembered that the probability of getting 3 insignificant values out of 31 may be quite high, i.e., under the alternative hypothesis that $\rho \neq 0$. More importantly, the values of ρ were all of the same sign and indeed they were mostly of the same order of magnitude. This was encouraging, since it suggested that the underlying processes governing the dynamics of the Entitled Electors were similar across counties.

All but one of the estimated constant terms were insignificant at the 5 per cent level. However, they were positively signed, as one might expect. Under the null hypothesis that they were all zero the probability that none of the estimates is significant at the 5 per cent level is about 0.2, so we accepted the hypothesis that they were all effectively zero, in the sense that they could be ignored for modelling purposes. For this reason we re-estimated the model described by (3.9) excluding the constant term. Details of the results of this exercise are also given in Table 3.1. It can be seen that the new estimates of $(\hat{\rho}_2)$ are only marginally different from the first set of estimates $(\hat{\rho}_1)$.

Having estimated this model for each county we were able to remove some of the stochastic element of ΔE_t as follows. For any county the fitted model is:

$$\Delta Z_t = -\hat{\alpha}\Delta Z_{t-1} + e_t$$

where $\hat{\alpha} = -\hat{\rho}_2$, as described above, and hence $0 < \alpha < 1$. We may write this as:

$$(Z_t - Z_{t-1}) = -\hat{\alpha}(Z_{t-1} - Z_{t-2}) + e_t$$
$$\text{or} \quad Z_t = (1 - \hat{\alpha})Z_{t-1} + \hat{\alpha}Z_{t-2} + e_t$$

where, as before, $Z_t = \Delta E_t$ is the flow of Entitled Electors. This equation yielded fitted values for these flows as:

$$\hat{Z}_t = (1 - \hat{\alpha})Z_{t-1} + \hat{\alpha}Z_{t-2} \qquad (3.10)$$

which is just a two point moving average. We then re-integrated the series to obtain fitted values for the stock (numbers) of Entitled Electors, i.e.,:

$$\hat{E}_t = R_{55} + \sum_{s=56}^{t} \hat{Z}_s = R_{55} + \sum_{s=56}^{t} \Delta\hat{E}_s$$

where R_{55} is the Register in 1955 and $\hat{Z}_2$ and $\hat{Z}_3$ were set to the value of $R_{56} - R_{55}$.

Table 3.1: *Estimates of the parameters of the proposed model with and without a constant term together with the t- statistics associated with the coefficients and R^2 for the second equation.*

Borough or County	With constant term				Without constant term		
	Constant	t	p_1	t	p_2	t	R^2
CORK BOROUGH	215.4	1.36	-0.421	-1.87	-0.391	-1.72	0.113
DUBLIN BOROUGH**	176.2	0.24	-0.451	-2.35*	-0.452	-2.43*	0.236
LIMERICK BOROUGH	60.5	0.50	-0.727	-5.06*	-0.725	-5.14*	0.534
WATERFORD BOROUGH	28.6	0.56	-0.687	-4.57*	-0.673	-4.61*	0.450
CARLOW	80.9	0.98	-0.340	-1.69	-0.325	-1.62	0.102
CAVAN	81.1	1.48	-0.728	-4.85*	-0.693	-4.58*	0.477
CLARE	153.6	0.77	-0.496	-2.50*	-0.490	-2.50*	0.213
CORK	306.2	0.88	-0.482	-2.58*	-0.466	-2.51*	0.215
DONEGAL	195.8	1.35	-0.796	-4.68*	-0.750	-4.43*	0.460
DUBLIN	1034.6	1.58	-0.649	-4.15*	-0.618	-3.86*	0.393
GALWAY	402.2	1.01	-0.547	-2.76*	-0.532	-2.69*	0.240
KERRY	116.8	0.54	-0.409	-2.15*	-0.403	-2.16*	0.168
KILDARE	304.0	1.40	-0.638	-3.71*	-0.619	-3.53*	0.352
KILKENNY	120.3	1.41	-0.784	-5.98*	-0.767	-5.75*	0.590
LAOIS	56.7	0.62	-0.482	-2.58*	-0.473	-2.57*	0.224
LEITRIM	33.8	0.55	-0.445	-2.37*	-0.441	-2.39*	0.199
LIMERICK	257.3	1.53	-0.725	-4.88*	-0.699	-4.60*	0.479
LONGFORD	60.7	0.93	-0.724	-4.80*	-0.710	-4.74*	0.494
LOUTH	114.7	0.74	-0.379	-1.95	-0.362	-1.89	0.135
MAYO	137.2	0.43	-0.747	-5.20*	-0.744	-5.28*	0.548
MEATH	221.5	2.69*	-0.880	-6.79*	-0.808	-5.65*	0.581
MONAGHAN	81.5	0.57	-0.680	-4.25*	-0.678	-4.30*	0.445
OFFALY	91.1	1.16	-0.446	-2.27*	-0.428	-2.17*	0.169
ROSCOMMON	84.9	0.73	-0.649	-3.94*	-0.644	-3.95*	0.404
SLIGO	113.2	0.94	-0.530	-2.95*	-0.520	-2.91*	0.269
TIPPERARY N.R.	74.4	0.67	-0.719	-4.16*	-0.704	-4.15*	0.429
TIPPERARY S.R.	84.3	0.46	-0.625	-3.16*	-0.626	-3.23*	0.312
WATERFORD	89.9	1.03	-0.739	-5.13*	-0.727	-5.06*	0.526
WESTMEATH	96.1	0.61	-0.631	-3.97*	-0.627	-4.00*	0.411
WEXFORD	151.1	1.02	-0.476	-2.46*	-0.457	-2.37*	0.196
WICKLOW	113.3	0.63	-0.791	-5.90*	-0.789	-5.96*	0.607

* Significant at the 5 per cent level.
** In view of our adjustments to the Dublin Borough Register for recent years we used only the years 1955 to 1976 to estimate this equation.

Apart from a constant term in $\hat{E}_t$, which is a result of the fact that $R_1 \neq E_1$, the effect of using these starting up values should "wash out" of the series fairly rapidly. In particular, the relative sizes of $\hat{E}_t$ between years should reflect the changes in the numbers of Entitled Electors. Details of the values of this series together with the associated flows and the original data (adjusted Registers) for the State as a whole are given in Table 3.2. The same series disaggregated to counties are given in Appendix E.

Direct Calculation of the Fitted Values of Entitled Electors

This section describes a way in which the fitted values and flows of the Entitled Electors may be calculated directly from the data on the Register. Two equations from the previous sections are relevant.

Table 3.2: *Registers (adjusted), Fitted Numbers of Entitled Electors and Fitted Flows of Entitled Electors, 1957 to 1982 for the State.*

Year	Register (Adjusted)*	Entitled Electors (fitted)	Flows of Entitled Electors (fitted)
1957	1,903,342	1,897,595	-24,447
1958	1,876,350	1,876,927	-20,668
1959	1,856,543	1,853,769	-23,161
1960	1,848,946	1,830,027	-23,738
1961	1,845,049	1,820,425	-9,605
1962	1,844,204	1,818,240	-2,182
1963	1,842,726	1,817,640	-600
1964	1,851,491	1,816,597	-1,048
1965	1,870,620	1,821,055	4,459
1966	1,883,127	1,840,627	19,571
1967	1,890,259	1,857,243	16,620
1968	1,895,820	1,865,065	7,820
1969	1,916,787	1,869,647	4,583
1970	1,928,966	1,884,927	15,276
1971	1,944,640	1,904,024	19,099
1972	1,973,084	1,915,980	11,953
1973	1,998,149	1,940,830	24,853
1974	2,023,856	1,970,261	29,430
1975	2,050,043	1,994,901	24,637
1976	2,082,231	2,020,559	25,658
1977	2,125,541	2,050,939	30,378
1978	2,150,190	2,090,892	39,954
1979	2,192,292	2,126,506	35,609
1980	2,224,180	2,155,499	28,995
1981	2,261,750	2,196,962	41,462
1982	2,310,180	2,228,531	31,569

*This is the Register after the adjustments described in Appendix A have been made to it.

Using our approximation to ΔE_t from equation (3.8):

$$\Delta E_t = \frac{1}{\Theta}(\Delta R_t - (1-\Theta)\,\Delta R_{t-1})$$

which may be written:

$$\Theta\Delta E_t = \Delta R_t - (1-\Theta)\Delta R_{t-1}$$

From the last section (equation 3.10) we also have:

$$\Delta\hat{E}_{t+1} = (1-\hat{\alpha})\,\Delta E_t + \hat{\alpha}\Delta E_{t-1}$$

Hence:

$$\Theta\Delta\hat{E}_{t+1} = (1-\hat{\alpha})\Theta\Delta E_t + \hat{\alpha}\,\Theta\,\Delta E_{t-1}$$
$$= (1-\hat{\alpha})\,(\Delta R_t - (1-\Theta)\,\Delta R_{t-1})$$
$$+ \hat{\alpha}\,(\Delta R_{t-1} - (1-\Theta)\,\Delta R_{t-2})$$

Letting $\hat{\beta} = (1-\hat{\alpha})$ and expanding:

$$\Theta\Delta\hat{E}_{t+1} = \hat{\beta}R_t + (-2\hat{\beta}+\hat{\beta}\Theta+\hat{\alpha})\,R_{t-1}$$
$$+ (\hat{\beta}-\hat{\beta}\,\Theta - 2\hat{\alpha}+\hat{\alpha}\Theta)\,R_{t-2}$$
$$+ (\hat{\alpha}-\hat{\alpha}\Theta)\,R_{t-3}$$

or

$$\Delta\hat{E}_{t+1} = w_0 R_t + w_1 R_{t-1} + w_2 R_{t-2} + w_3 R_{t-3}$$

where:

$$w_0 = \hat{\beta}/\Theta$$
$$w_1 = (-2\hat{\beta}+\hat{\beta}\Theta+\hat{\alpha})/\Theta$$
$$w_2 = (\hat{\beta}-\hat{\beta}\Theta-2\hat{\alpha}+\hat{\alpha}\Theta)/\Theta$$
$$w_3 = (\hat{\alpha}-\hat{\alpha}\Theta)/\Theta$$

Thus, given the most recent four values of the Register (in some county), it is only necessary to evaluate the above expression in order to obtain the appropriate fitted flow value. The value of Θ is 0.6692 for all counties. The values of $\hat{\alpha}$, and hence $\hat{\beta}$, are different for each county. Table 3.3 gives the appropriate values of w_0, w_1, w_2 and w_3 for each county. Once $\Delta\hat{E}_{t+1}$ has been calculated, $\hat{E}_{t+1}$, the fitted values of Entitled Electors may be calculated by the relationship

$$\hat{E}_{t+1} = \hat{E}_t + \Delta\hat{E}_{t+1}$$

where (as described in the previous section):

$$\hat{E}_{55} = R_{55} \text{ and } \Delta\hat{E}_{56} = \Delta\hat{E}_{57} = R_{56} - R_{55}.$$

Two interesting points may be noted about the weights w_0, w_1, w_2, w_3. First, it is easy to show that:

$$w_0 + w_1 + w_2 + w_3 = 0$$

Thus, if $\Delta R_t = 0$ for four years in succession then $\Delta\hat{E}_t = 0$. In other words if the size of the Register settles down to a constant so does the fitted value of the Entitled Electors. Secondly:

$$4w_0 + 3w_1 + 2w_2 + w_3 = 1$$

Hence, if the Register continues to grow by a constant amount each year then eventually so does the fitted Entitled Electors series, since if

$$R_t = R_{t-1} + C, R_{t+1} = R_{t-1} + 2C,.$$
$$R_{t+2} = R_{t-1} + 3C, R_{t+3} = R_{t-1} + 4C,$$

then,

$$\Delta\hat{E}_{t+5} = w_0 (R_{t-1} + 4C) + w_1(R_{t-1} + 3C)$$
$$+ w_2 (R_{t-1} + 2C) + w_3 (R_{t-1} + C)$$
$$= (w_0 + w_1 + w_2 + w_3) R_{t-1} + (4w_0 + 3w_1 + 2w_2 + w_3)C$$
$$= C$$

These two properties of the weights mean that our Entitled Elector series must eventually reflect the properties of the Register. It is completely in keeping with our finding that the errors of the Register are a result of turnover of the Register that this should be the case.

Conclusion

The construction of these smoothed estimates of the Entitled Elector and their flows effectively realises the purpose of this chapter, namely, the production of a data set suitable for the construction of independent variables in a regression analysis involving time series data. Although the model used to do this might be described as naive, its efficacy in the above context seems

Table 3.3: *Values of the weights W_0 W_1 W_2 and W_3 to be used for computing the fitted values of the flows of Entitled Electors given for each county.*

| County | Weights | | | |
	W_0	W_1	W_2	W_3
CORK BOROUGH	0.91004	-0.62680	-0.47652	0.19328
DUBLIN BOROUGH	0.81889	-0.41434	-0.62798	0.22343
LIMERICK BOROUGH	0.41094	0.53651	-1.30583	0.35838
WATERFORD BOROUGH	0.48864	0.35539	-1.17671	0.33268
CARLOW	1.00867	-0.85668	-0.31264	0.16065
CAVAN	0.45876	0.42505	-1.22637	0.34256
CLARE	0.76210	-0.28199	-0.72233	0.24222
CORK	0.79797	-0.36558	-0.66274	0.23035
DONEGAL	0.37358	0.62358	-1.36790	0.37074
DUBLIN	0.57083	0.16383	-1.04015	0.30549
GALWAY	0.69934	-0.13571	-0.82662	0.26298
KERRY	0.89211	-0.58501	-0.50631	0.19921
KILDARE	0.56934	0.16731	-1.04263	0.30599
KILKENNY	0.34818	0.68279	-1.41011	0.37914
LAOIS	0.78751	-0.34120	-0.68012	0.23381
LEITRIM	0.83533	-0.45266	-0.60067	0.21800
LIMERICK	0.44979	0.44595	-1.23127	0.34553
LONGFORD	0.43335	0.48426	-1.26858	0.35097
LOUTH	0.95338	-0.72781	-0.40451	0.17894
MAYO	0.38254	0.60268	-1.35300	0.36778
MEATH	0.28691	0.82559	-1.51191	0.39941
MONAGHAN	0.48117	0.37281	-1.18913	0.33515
OFFALY	0.85475	-0.49793	-0.56839	0.21570
ROSCOMMON	0.53198	0.25439	-1.10471	0.31834
SLIGO	0.71727	-0.17750	-0.79682	0.25705
TIPPERARY N.R.	0.44232	0.46336	-1.25369	0.34800
TIPPERARY S.R.	0.55888	0.19169	-1.06001	0.30945
WATERFORD	0.40795	0.54347	-1.31079	0.35937
WESTMEATH	0.55738	0.19518	-1.06250	0.30994
WEXFORD	0.81142	-0.39693	-0.64039	0.22590
WICKLOW	0.31530	0.75942	-1.46474	0.39002

sufficient. As the reader shall see, in the next chapter, use of the series in the model for population estimation developed there does indeed overcome the problem of a highly variable derived migration series referred to at the start of the present chapter. The models fitted to equation (3.9) also serve another function. These models may be used for tracking the series, that is comparing one step ahead forecasts with the corresponding realised value. Large deviations between two such values would expose changes of procedure on the part of the Registration authorities such as that which created the Dublin stockpile. As such we have a safeguard against being taken unawares by structural changes in the Register.

Chapter 4

POPULATION ESTIMATION

This chapter examines the extent to which the Register may be used to make estimates of population. Our main idea is based on the so-called 'ratio-correlation' method of population estimation (see Namboodiri, 1972) in which the correlation between growth, or decline, in population levels and growth in some variable symptomatic of population is exploited. A symptomatic variable is usually constituted by the number of persons in some subset of the population which may be expected to form a constant proportion of the population, (for example, car owners or school enrolments) and which is measured more regularly than the population itself. The ratio-correlation method seeks to determine the form of the relationship between the population and the symptomatic variable at times when both variables are known and then use this to make estimates of population at times when only the symptomatic variable is known. The general methodology of the ratio-correlation method is discussed in the second section of this chapter.

In the third section of the chapter we formulate a new ratio-correlation model for population estimation. Our plan here is to extend the work of Whelan and Keogh, (1980), which presented a model of the ratio-correlation type with the Register as the symptomatic variable. As we now have a good deal more information about the Register at our disposal, it should be possible to construct a better model. The Entitled Electors series, developed in Chapter 3, should constitute a more appropriate symptomatic variable since it represents numbers of persons aged 18 years and over resident in the State and is not distorted by the timing which affect the Register. It has also a certain stochastic component removed. Our new model also takes heed both of a point raised by Hughes, (1981), regarding the timing of the Census, and the extent to which the whole approach can be affected by changes in the age structure of the population. Using this model we are able to present a consistent set of regional population estimates for Ireland for the years 1961 to 1981. The migration series for each region which are implicit in the population estimates are also calculated.

Features of the migration series implicit in the population figures for the State as a whole are discussed in the fourth section of the chapter. We compare our new migration series with the series given in Whelan and Keogh (1980), and the series implicit in the CSO's population estimates. We find that the new series is a good deal less variable than the earlier series, but that all three series exhibit the same overall patterns over the period in question. Keenan (1981) has pointed out the importance of having good estimates of migration since this variable has important economic implications and the availability of such a series is a useful input into ecomometric model building exercises.

In the fifth section of the chapter we examine the extent to which our knowledge of the Register may be used to make estimates of current population levels, that is, population levels since the most recent Census in 1981. Unfortunately, whereas the ratio-correlation method is an adequate device for making estimates of historical population levels it is not appropriate for this latter exercise. The problem stems from the fact that changes in the age structure can radically affect the method. Nevertheless, we are able to make use of the Entitled Electors series by taking a somewhat different approach. Net migration amongst the population of Entitled Electors may be estimated by considering this population of persons in its own right and by using an adaption of the traditional fertility/mortality approach to population estimation applied to it[21]. Some indications of recent migration trends and hence recent population levels may be gleaned in this way.

The Ratio Correlation Method

A brief outline of the ratio-correlation method is given here. The idea is developed in two steps. Denote the population to be estimated by P and the symptomatic variable by S. Let P_T be the population to be estimated in year T and let S_T be the known value of the symptomatic variable in year T. Finally let P_c and S_c be the known values of P and S in some census year different from year T. If the ratio of P to S is constant in all years we may note that $P_T/S_T = P_c/S_c$ and hence:

$$P_T = (P_T/S_T). S_T = (P_c/S_c). S_T$$

As both of the terms on the right hand side are known, P_T, is then also known. The general idea of the ratio correlation method is that provided the ratio of P to S stays reasonably stable we may use the P_c/S_c as a proxy for P_T/S_T. More exactly we are writing:

$$\text{Estimate of } P_T = [\text{Estimate of } (P_T/S_T)] .S_T$$

where the estimate of P_T/S_T is P_c/S_c.

---

[21]This approach, fertility/mortality, to population forecasting has been used in Ireland by Knaggs and Keane (1971), Keating (1976) and Blackwell and McGregor (1982).

This is essentially the approach taken in Whelan and Keogh (1980). It may be called the 'raw-ratio' method.

A more elaborate method of estimating P_T is given by:

$$\text{Estimate of } P_T = [\text{Estimate of } (P_T/P_c)] \ P_c$$

where Estimate of $(P_T/P_c) = \alpha + \beta \ (S_T/S_c)$ with suitable values of α and β. This method assumes that the growth rates in the population and in the symptomatic variable are linearly related but not necessarily equal. The constant term α represents growth in the population which is independent of growth in the symptomatic variable. The slope, β, takes into account the fact that growth in S may over-represent or under-represent growth in P. Note that in the case $\alpha = 0$, $\beta = 1$ this reduces to the raw-ratio method. The ratio-correlation approach is to estimate α and β by linear regression when values of (P_T/P_c) and (S_T/S_c) are known at two or more times and over several regions. The methodology of this paper goes one stage further. Recognizing that the linear relationship between the growth rates in the two variables in question may itself be subject to changes, we define a model which allows the parameters α and β to vary across time.

Population Estimation

In this section we shall attempt to bring together the elements of our analysis so far to obtain a set of consistent annual regional population figures for the years 1961 to 1981. As outlined in the previous section the idea is simple enough, we relate the numbers of Entitled Electors to the numbers in the population as a whole in census years and then use this relationship to estimate population figures for non-census years. Our model uses the data on the Entitled Electors derived in Chapter 3 and the county populations as given in the Censuses of Population for 1956, 1961, 1966, 1971, 1979 and 1981[22]. The model was constructed with the following ideas in mind:

(i)   The data on the Entitled Electors derived in Chapter 3 should be more representative of actual population on any given date than the Register data, as the former data has been largely purged of the influence of the lags which affect the reported numbers on the Register. Furthermore, the model fitting exercise carried out in the last chapter will also have removed some of the stochastic component of these data, rendering them more suitable for use as an independent variable in a regression model.

(ii) Hughes (1981) pointed out that there is a discrepancy between the month to which the Register refers and the month in which the census is carried

[22]The 1981 census data used in constructing the model was taken from the Preliminary Report. This differs marginally from the data in Volume I which has been subsequently published.

out. This is equally true of the Entitled Elector series since although we have removed the lag effects between this series and the Register, the series still refers to September and hence there is still a timing difference between it and the census. A solution to this problem may be obtained by forming interpolates of the Entitled Electors across pairs of adjacent years. Hopefully this will be more representative of the population at census time. However, it is not clear in what proportions the interpolations should be made. A fifty-fifty combination of two successive years appears a likely candidate, as the census time is April which is just about half way between the two September dates to which such Entitled Elector figures would refer. But this approach assumes that the flows of Entitled Electors are evenly spread across a year and it is by no means clear that this is the case. To overcome this problem we attempted to estimate the appropriate interpolation proportion as part of the model.

(iii)   Even if the above mentioned problems involving the compatibility of the data have been solved, the relationshhip between the Entitled Electors and the population as a whole may have been changing over time. For example in 1966 the percentage of persons aged 18 years and over was 63.1 per cent, whereas in 1981 it was 63.8 per cent. The difference in percentage terms of 0.7 per cent may seem small but it amounts to about 24,000 persons in 1981. Thus we wished to parameterize our model in such a way as to accommodate structural change. This approach also satisfies the principle of parsimony, i.e., use of as few parameters as possible to describe the relationship between the variables. The original model described in Whelan and Keogh (1980) involved 23 parameters, the present model has less than a half of that number. As the predictive value of the present model is similar to that of the previous model we felt that an improvement had been made.

We will denote the fitted values of the Entitled Electors series in county i and year t by E_{it}. The corresponding population, when t is a census year, will be denoted P_{it}. The value of the fitted net flow of Entitled Electors between years $t-1$ and t in county i is denoted $Z_{it} = E_{it} - E_{it-1}$. The Register in any year refers to a date in the September of the previous calendar year and, as we have used the same dating convention, this is also true of the Entitled Electors. Thus an estimate of the number of Entitled Electors present in April of year t is given by:

$$G_{it+1} = E_{it+1} - \gamma Z_{it+1}   0 < \gamma < 1 \tag{4.1}$$

[23]In this chapter we have dropped the hats ` ^ ` for typographical convenience. They are no longer necessary as we work exclusively with fitted values of the Entitled Electors.

where γ is appropriately chosen. For example, if all registration authorities rigidly adhered to the 15th September as the qualification date, and if the flows of Entitled Electors (Z_{it}) are evenly spread across the registration year then an estimate of the numbers of Entitled Electors present in county i on 1 April of year t is given by:

$$G_{it+1} = E_{it+1} - (168/365) Z_{it+1}$$

as there are 168 days between 1 April and 15 September. Here we have taken the numbers of Entitled Electors which have been dated (indexed) as $t + 1$, and hence refer to September of year t, and subtracted a proportion (168/365) of the flow between September of year $t-1$ and September of year t, the proportion being chosen to correspond to that part of flow which occurred after 1 April. But, of course, we do not know that the flow is evenly spread across the year. Thus in accordance with aim (ii) outlined above we shall allow γ to be determined within the estimation procedure. With this understood G_{it+1}, as described in equation (4.1), is our symptomatic variable. Following the approach outlined in the last section we specified our model as:

$$\left(\frac{P_{it}}{P_{iB}}\right) = \alpha_t + \beta_t \left(\frac{E_{it+1} - \gamma Z_{it+1}}{E_{iB+1} - \gamma Z_{iB+1}}\right) \qquad i=1...,31 \qquad (4.2)$$

where the base year B was chosen to be the census year 1956, and t runs across the census years 1961, 1971, 1979 and 1981. The model enbodies two hypotheses. The first is that the growth in population between the base year, B, and the census year, t, is linearly related, across counties, to growth in the symptomatic variable over the same period. The second is that the parameters describing the relationship, α_t and β_t, differ from one census year to another. The first hypothesis acknowledges the fact that growth in the symptomatic variable may under-represent or over-represent changes in the population as a whole, the second allows for the fact that the degree to which this phenomenon is present may itself change from year to year. These features of the model reflect our third aim described at the start of the section.

When γ is fixed, equation (4.2) above becomes a linear regression model with 10 parameters, that is, a pair of parameters for each of the five census years in question. In view of this the model was estimated by a grid search across various values of γ. For each value of γ from 0 to 1 in steps of 1/12 the corresponding linear regression model with 10 coefficients was estimated. The model with the lowest estimated residual variance was then chosen[24]. It was

[24]Models which have the property that they become linear when a parameter which must lie between two given bounds is fixed are often estimated in this way. See Schmidt (1976).

revealing to plot the values of these estimated variances against the corresponding values of γ. This is done in Fig. 4.1, which shows that a genuine global minimum exists at $\gamma = 3/12$ and as γ runs from 0 to 1 the fit of the model becomes progressively better up to that point and progressively worse after it. Thus the appropriate proportion of the flow to subtract from the numbers of Entitled Electors is ¼.

The estimated values of α_t and β_t for each of the relevant census years, together with their associated t values and other regression statistics are given for the model with $\gamma = $ ¼ in Table 4.1. It is noticeable that the slope coefficients are all greater than 1 and that they rise slowly between the years 1961 and 1979. This indicates that growth in the numbers of Entitled Electors under-represented growth in the population as a whole because growth in the former variable has to be scaled up to be on par with growth in the latter variable. This suggests that the age group of those under 18 years grew more rapidly than the age group of those aged 18 years and over and this generally agrees with the information on the age structure available from the census. Also the phenomenon became increasingly more pronounced over the period 1961 to 1979. This trend appears to have been reversed between 1979 and 1981. It should be remembered that the coefficients given in any row of Table 4.1 will

Figure 4.1: *Estimated Variances for the model described by equation (4.2) for each fixed value of γ between 0 and 1 in steps of 1/12.*

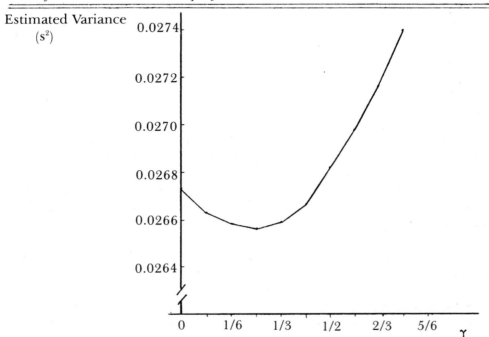

Table 4.1: *Estimates of the parameters in the model described by equation (4.2) with γ set at 3/12 together with associated regression statistics.*

Year	α_t	t statistic	β_t	t statistic
1961	0.0	—	1.01498	191.270
1966	-0.11434	-2.037	1.13136	19.374
1971	-0.12599	-3.672	1.14546	33.039
1979	-0.16255	-8.018	1.17722	65.820
1981	-0.16715	-9.032	1.16332	74.443

$R^2 = 0.99943$

Table 4.2: *Populations, fitted populations and the associated fitting error for each census year together with the corresponding errors from the model estimated in Whelan and Keogh (1980).*

Year	Population (1)	Fitted Population (2)	Error (3) = (1) − (2)	Error in WK (1980)
1961	2,818,341	2,811,660	6,681	7,637
1966	2,884,002	2,864,569	19,433	5,242
1971	2,978,248	2,977,299	949	1,893
1979	3,368,217	3,388,588	-20,371	-17,092
1981	3,440,427	3,458,534	-18,107	—

depend on the difference between the growth in the population and the growth in the number of Entitled Electors over the period from the base year (1956) to the census year with which these coefficients are associated. Thus if at sometime within that period the population was growing more slowly than the Entitled Electors and at another time more rapidly, these effects will tend to cancel out. However, the fairly systematic way in which the coefficients changed over the whole period indicates that this type of effect is unlikely.

The R_2 value of 0.99943 shows that the model yields a very good fit by conventional standards but as we have already pointed out even very small discrepancies, such as that between the age structures in 1966 and 1981, can correspond to sizeable numbers of persons. Therefore, to determine how well this model fits in terms of numbers of persons, we obtained fitted values for the populations in each census year using the formula:

$$\hat{P}_{it} = \left(\hat{\alpha}_t + \hat{\beta}_t \frac{(E_{it+1} - \hat{\gamma}Z_{i, t+1})}{(E_{i, B+1} - \hat{\gamma}Z_{i, B+1})} \right) P_{iB} \qquad (4.3)$$

where $\hat{\gamma} = \frac{1}{4}$ and $\hat{\alpha}_t$ and $\hat{\beta}_t$ are the coefficients given in Table 4.1. In other words we multiply the estimated growth in population in county i between year B and year t by that county's population in year B. The results of this exercise for the State as a whole are given in Table 4.2. This table gives the actual and fitted populations for the various census years together with the errors incurred in the fitting procedure and the corresponding errors from the earlier Whelan and Keogh model.

The errors from the present model are slightly larger than those from the earlier one. Nevertheless, what difference is discernible seems a small price to pay for a reduction in the number of estimated parameters by over 50 per cent, from 23 to 11. In no year is the error greater than 0.7 per cent of the true population. Furthermore, it should be borne in mind that these errors are overall measures of fit and do not necessarily correspond to the errors that would be made using the model in practice. We also have a model in which each of the parameters has a definite interpretation and, as we shall show in the sequel, the new model generates a much more realistic implied migration series. That there was a problem regarding the volatile nature of the migration series described in Whelan and Keogh (1980) was recognized in that article and further discussed in Hughes (1981) and Keenan (1982).

The model described by equation (4.2) may be used to determine a consistent set of regional populations over the years 1961 to 1981. Unlike the basic ratio correlation method, in which only one intercept and one slope would be estimated using two census years, we have an intercept and a scope for each census year. Assuming the parameter γ is fixed we in fact have five models corresponding to the basic ratio correlation method applied to 1956 paired with each of the census years between 1961 and 1981 inclusive. The situation is depicted in Fig. 4.2. The values of the parameters to be used when fitting the model in census years have been given in Table 4.1. However it is not clear what values of these parameters are appropriate for intercensal years, precisely the years in which the method is useful. For example, for the year 1963, we could use α_1 and β_1, which is the way the ratio correlation approach would be used between 1961 and 1966 when only the data for 1956 and 1961 was available. But we could also use α_2 and β_2, which contain information about two years straddling the year in question.

We decided on the following approach to the problem. As the values of α_t and β_t in census year t embody information about the divergence between

Figure 4.2: *Schematic Representation of the periods to which the coefficients in the model apply*

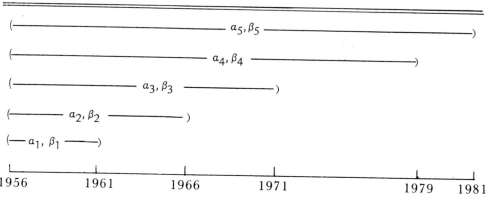

growth rates in population and growth rates in Entitled Electors between 1956 and that census year, and as it is reasonable to assume that the extent of this divergence changes slowly and continuously (since it is the result of demographic forces, in particular the age structure) some form of interpolation procedure would seem appropriate. This is equivalent to assuming that in any year t, not necessarily a census year, there exist values of α_t and β_t for which:

$$\frac{P_{it}}{P_{iB}} = \alpha_t + \beta_t \left(\frac{E_{i,t+1} - \gamma Z_{i,t+1}}{E_{i,B+1} - \gamma Z_{i,B+1}} \right) \qquad (4.4)$$

would be the appropriate model and that α_t and β_t are continuous functions of time, t. We, of course, have been able to estimate α_t and β_t for census years only. We decided to use Lagrange interpolating polynomials for α_t and β_t across the time period involved and these are depicted in Figure 4.3 and Figure 4.4 respectively[25]. As there were five values of each parameter this amounted to fitting quartic polynomials. It is easy to see from this figure that even a simple piecewise linear interpolation between the various values of α_t and β_t would have given similar results. However as the Lagrange procedure is well known and yields a single formula for the interpolating function we chose it in preference to any other method. The fitted polynomials for α_t and β_t are defined by:

[25]The reader who is familiar with linear regression theory will note that this procedure is equivalent to substituting polynomials for α_t and β_t in equation (4.2) and then estimating the coefficients of these polynomials directly, that is, a reparameterization of the column space of the independent variables.

Figure 4.3: *Interpolating polynomial for the intercept coefficient* α_t

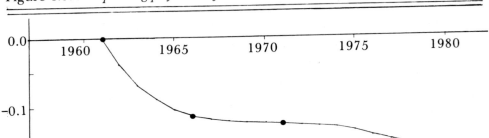

Figure 4.4: *Interpolating coefficient for the slope coefficient* β_t

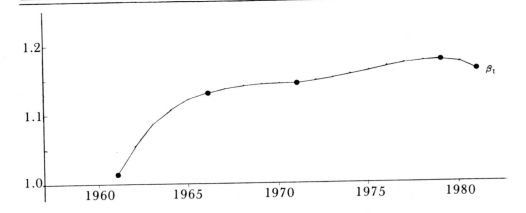

$$\alpha_{t-1} = -0.46084t + 0.63136t^2 - 0.37166t^3 + 0.075147t^4$$

$$\beta_{t-1} = 1.01498 + 0.48308t - 0.69801t^2 + 0.44403t^3 - 0.09863t^4 \qquad (4.5)$$

where a unit of time corresponds to a decade and the origin, $t = 0$, was fixed at 1962. Note that these formulae give α_{t-1} and β_{t-1}. This is only done for computational convenience since we must multiply the β_t by values made up from the number of Entitled Electors dated in time as referring to the year after the year in which we wish to fit population values.

Using the coefficients fitted in this way and the variables E_{it} and Z_{it} we were able to obtain fitted values for county populations for all years between 1961 and 1981. These have been aggregated up to regions in Table 4.3. In terms of all the foregoing analysis the method used to do this was in four stages:

(i)   Determine the values of α_t and β_t appropriate to the year in question using the polynomials in equation (4.5).

Table 4.3: *Fitted populations for the years 1961 to 1981 given by planning region and for the State as a whole.*

Year	East	North East	South East	South West	Mid West	West	Midlands	North West and Donegal	State[1]
				Planning Region					
1961	895,185	173,565	321,273	446,273	261,878	273,171	237,162	203,153	2,811,660
1962	902,301	173,086	319,937	444,840	261,885	270,818	235,019	202,004	2,809,889
1963	914,530	171,878	318,170	442,265	161,019	267,551	232,275	199,409	2,807,097
1964	924,688	168,505	318,328	442,338	261,947	265,939	231,783	196,799	2,810,327
1965	940,043	167,833	321,798	446,773	265,491	264,580	232,925	196,342	2,835,786
1966	959,792	169,175	322,584	451,292	267,267	267,136	232,086	195,236	2,864,569
1967	978,559	168,811	322,968	451,750	269,560	264,552	231,141	194,285	2,881,626
1968	992,796	169,106	324,556	452,150	269,773	260,542	229,823	192,944	2,891,690
1969	1,011,941	169,733	326,740	455,573	270,850	259,805	228,868	191,845	2,915,354
1970	1,035,893	171,345	329,765	459,368	272,583	260,669	228,824	191,279	2,949,726
1971	1,055,353	173,175	330,950	463,268	274,848	259,966	228,663	191,076	2,977,299
1972	1,078,258	175,097	334,709	470,260	277,850	260,560	230,501	192,114	3,019,349
1973	1,106,858	177,197	339,749	478,148	281,301	262,918	233,782	193,538	3,073,492
1974	1,133,676	180,003	343,935	485,021	284,835	265,692	235,404	194,578	3,123,143
1975	1,161,055	182,910	348,068	491,528	287,932	267,927	236,506	195,286	3,171,211
1976	1,190,069	186,658	352,476	498,590	291,360	271,513	237,544	195,945	3,224,155
1977	1,220,006	190,161	357,622	508,329	294,961	279,012	240,557	198,352	3,289,000
1978	1,249,037	191,922	363,520	514,707	297,857	284,447	244,856	201,344	3,347,690
1979	1,266,857	193,128	368,826	518,999	301,735	286,959	248,639	203,446	3,388,588
1980	1,285,772	195,170	375,511	524,263	303,679	291,237	252,742	205,456	3,433,831
1981	1,297,121	196,497	378,833	527,505	304,712	293,671	253,788	206,406	3,458,534

[1]Totals may not add due to rounding.

(ii)   Using these values of α_t and β_t estimate the growth in population between 1956 and year t in each county by:

$$\hat{g}_{it} = \text{Estimate of growth in county i's population}$$
$$= \alpha_t + \beta_t \left(\frac{E_{i, t+1} - \gamma Z_{i, t+1}}{E_{i, B+1} - \gamma Z_{i, B+1}} \right)$$

where $\gamma = \frac{1}{4}$ and B + 1 corresponds to 1957.

(iii)   The fitted population for county i in year t is then:

$$\hat{P}_{it} = \hat{g}_{it} \cdot P_{iB}$$

(iv)   Aggregate the fitted population for counties into regions.

These estimates suffer from the defect that they do not correspond exactly to the Census data in census years. As a final cosmetic exercise we fitted cubic splines, considered as functions of time, to the relatively small divergences between the census values and the fitted values. The values of the splines at non-census years were then subtracted from the fitted values to yield a slightly amended set of regional estimates with the property that they matched the census data exactly in census years. The final set of figures are presented in Table 4.4.

Migration

Given the fitted populations in Table 4.4 it is possible to compute the associated regional net migrations across each of the years from 1961 to 1981, using the known figures for births and deaths in these regions across the period. Net migration is, of course, the residual change in population from one year to the next when account has been taken of the natural increase, births less deaths. The migration series are given in Table 4.5. As envisaged at the outset these new migration estimates partially overcome a problem considered in the penultimate section of Whelan and Keogh (1980), namely, the high variability of the national net migration series derived in that paper. There it was suggested that using a moving average of the fitted populations to derive the migration estimates might alleviate the problem. In effect this has been done, but in terms of the Register itself. The reduction in 'noisyness' achieved can be seen in Figure 4.5, where the present series (RC), the original Whelan and Keogh series (WK) and the net migration series implicit in the Central Statistics Office's post censal population estimates (CSO) are graphed. These series are also given in Table 4.6. Below each series we have given the associated value of the von Neumann Ratio statistic. This statistic is conventionally used to test the hypothesis that a series is composed entirely of white noise, that is, that no correlation exists between successive terms of the

Table 4.4: *Fitted populations for the years 1961 to 1981 after the adjustments described in the text.*

Year	East	North East	South East	South West	Mid West	West	Midlands	North West and Donegal	State[1]
1961	906,347	171,060	319,883	446,901	260,737	273,217	239,323	200,873	2,818,341
1962	920,388	171,255	318,029	445,532	260,578	269,779	237,117	198,943	2,821,621
1963	937,904	170,644	315,837	443,045	259,496	265,640	234,360	195,701	2,822,628
1964	951,712	167,791	315,665	443,232	260,158	263,369	233,905	192,577	2,828,408
1965	969,079	167,563	318,899	447,806	263,386	261,564	235,132	191,738	2,855,167
1966	989,202	169,273	319,542	452,488	264,797	263,887	234,429	190,384	2,884,002
1967	1,006,705	169,200	319,877	453,134	266,675	261,283	233,669	189,318	2,899,862
1968	1,018,041	169,710	321,511	453,748	266,423	257,466	232,586	187,995	2,907,479
1969	1,032,647	170,475	323,834	457,409	266,985	257,135	231,915	187,047	2,927,447
1970	1,052,038	172,136	327,003	461,340	268,322	258,334	232,125	186,717	2,958,015
1971	1,062,067	173,964	328,604	465,655	269,804	258,748	232,427	186,979	2,978,248
1972	1,077,136	175,782	332,695	472,833	272,311	260,103	234,618	188,519	3,013,997
1973	1,099,494	177,676	337,983	480,679	275,555	262,865	238,142	190,482	3,062,876
1974	1,121,665	180,174	342,334	487,281	279,170	265,688	239,896	192,098	3,108,306
1975	1,145,992	182,672	346,547	493,288	282,637	267,616	241,020	193,418	3,153,189
1976	1,173,549	185,908	350,952	499,622	286,723	270,538	241,969	194,726	3,203,987
1977	1,203,623	188,797	356,010	508,404	291,270	277,017	244,784	197,819	3,267,725
1978	1,232,321	190,252	361,350	514,485	295,489	281,663	248,848	201,241	3,325,649
1979	1,255,533	190,231	366,788	516,474	300,802	281,857	252,137	204,395	3,368,217
1980	1,277,304	191,763	372,747	520,984	304,645	284,634	255,784	206,909	3,414,770
1981	1,288,973	193,296	374,484	525,022	208,040	286,384	256,413	207,815	3,440,427

Planning Region

[1]Totals may not add due to rounding.

Table 4.5: Net migration for the years 1962 to 1981 (April of previous year to April of the stated year) by planning region and for the State as a whole.

Year	East	North East	South East	South West	Mid West	West	Midlands	North West and Dongal	State[1]
				Planning Regions					
1962	1,144	-1,220	-4,667	-4,842	-2,258	-4,901	-4,110	-2,629	-23,483
1963	4,074	-2,104	-5,182	-6,117	-3,399	-5,947	-4,640	-4,026	-27,342
1964	-722	-4,415	-3,464	-3,546	-1,825	-4,108	-2,596	-4,264	-24,941
1965	2,180	-1,598	-98	879	581	-3,613	-924	-1,811	-4,405
1966	6,237	188	-2,271	717	-1,013	550	-2,703	-312	-2,016
1967	3,395	-1,571	-2,722	-3,177	-711	-4,231	-2,757	-1,910	-18,683
1968	-2,439	-1,237	-1,363	-3,831	-2,591	-5,201	-2,884	-2,343	-21,889
1969	743	-615	-543	325	-1,568	-1,844	-2,580	-1,670	-7,751
1970	4,792	231	-150	78	-1,108	-193	-1,528	-839	1,284
1971	-6,441	227	-2,012	-105	-1,103	-1,238	-1,739	-513	-12,924
1972	-1,508	-93	535	2,481	-360	-566	181	495	1,165
1973	4,987	250	1,580	3,084	86	790	1,608	954	13,339
1974	5,533	786	767	2,071	638	770	-261	619	10,924
1975	7,908	826	535	1,646	656	-92	-718	251	11,012
1976	11,462	1,458	628	1,726	1,205	724	-989	28	16,241
1977	14,589	1,080	1,355	4,116	1,390	4,404	907	1,913	29,755
1978	12,050	-466	1,657	1,742	1,289	2,249	2,033	1,989	22,542
1979	5,774	-2,017	1,436	-2,994	1,682	-2,357	1,161	1,800	4,485
1980	3,706	-556	1,495	-929	-29	500	1,044	778	6,009
1981	-6,233	-895	-2,618	-1,014	-331	-1,117	-1,877	-547	-14,632

[1]Totals may not add due to rounding.

Table 4.6: *Different estimates of net migration, 1962 to 1981 together with the von Neumann ratio values described in the text.*

Year	$(1)^1$	$(2)^2$	$(3)^3$
	'000		
1962	-23.5	-26.8	-14.9
1963	-27.3	-32.5	- 8.2
1964	-24.9	-13.3	-16.2
1965	- 4.4	- 1.0	-19.5
1966	- 0.3	- 4.5	-20.6
1967	-13.7	-19.2	-13.4
1968	-21.9	-20.0	-15.7
1969	- 7.8	5.6	-15.0
1970	1.3	- 9.6	- 5.5
1971	-12.9	- 8.4	- 4.3
1972	1.2	10.0	10.7
1973	13.3	- 1.6	12.8
1974	10.9	20.3	16.3
1975	11.0	4.9	19.1
1976	16.2	17.1	15.4
1977	29.8	47.2	9.0
1978	22.5	- 7.3	6.6
1979	4.5	31.1	15.9
1980	6.0	—	- 7.6
1981	-14.6	—	- 1.2
von Neumann ratio value	0.53	1.26	0.37

[1]Estimates implicit in the Ratio-correlation method.
[2]Whelan and Keogh's estimates.
[3]Central Statistics Office.

series. In the present context we are not proposing it as a formal test statistic, nevertheless, it does act as a useful summary measure of the degree of noisyness in any of the series. Values close to 2 suggest pure white noise, lower values indicate the presence of serial correlation and hence that the series is smoother. The value of the statistic (0.53) for the new series is about 45 per cent higher than that of the migration series implicit in the C.S.O.'s population series (0.37), whereas the value of the statistic for the WK series is 3½ times as large. It should be pointed out, of course, that smoothness in itself is not an

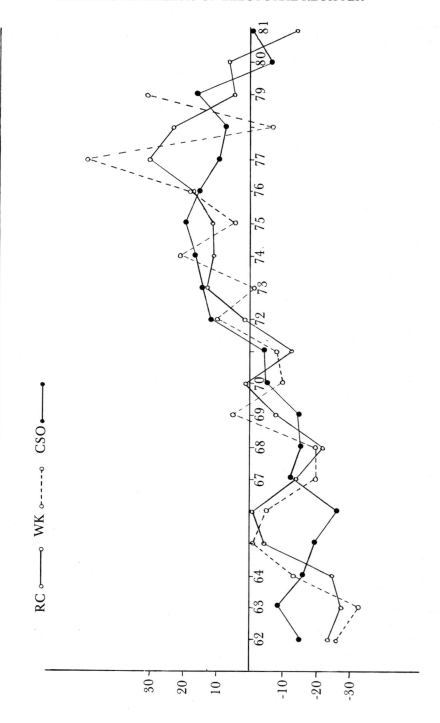

Figure 4.5: Net migration in thousands as implied by the population estimates given by (i) the ratio-correlation method (ii) Whelan and Keogh and (iii) the C.S.O. for the years ending in April 1962 to April 1981.

absolute criterion, since there is no reason to suppose that migration does not have some stochastic component. It is an entirely subjective view that the derived migration series should exhibit some tendency towards smoothness. On the other hand, it is difficult to believe that from one year to the next migratory behaviour can change drastically, if for no other reason than that the economic conditions which provoke migration do not change particularly rapidly.

All these series show a similar pattern over the two decades, with net emigration prevailing during the first decade, net immigration during the second decade and a return towards net emigration towards the end of the period. The value of the migration series derived from the Register is that it provides independent information about the distribution of migration across the years between censuses based on a regularly measured variable. Furthermore such information is available on a regional basis.

Estimation of current population

The previous sections of this chapter dealt with the estimation of past population levels. In the present section we consider the extent to which current population estimates may be made using the Register, that is, population estimates for the years between that of the most recent census and the current year. There is an important difference between these two exercises. In the case of the fitted past population values presented above, for any given year we know the census population values for a pair of years straddling the year in question. Thus, if the relationship between the population as a whole and the Register has changed over the period (due, for exmple, to a change in the age structure or the error structure of the Register) we have information to this effect. Furthermore, the varying parameters device used in our model will automatically take account of such changes. On the other hand, there is no information about structural changes which have occurred since the most recent census. Although we made several attempts based on the ratio correlation approach to get over this difficulty, none was fully successful.

There is, however, a different way in which the results of Chapters 2 and 3 can be used to obtain information about migration flows over the years in question. In Chapter 2 we noted that the population of Entitled Electors is, in theory, the population of persons aged 18 years and over. In Chapter 3 we provided a method of estimating the numbers of Entitled Electors and the net flow sizes of this group. The natural increase in this population in any year is the difference between the numbers of persons who became 18 years of age in that year and the numbers of persons aged 18 years and over who die during the year. Using Vol. II of the 1981 Census it was possible to determine the number of people who should have become 18 years of age in each of the subsequent years, the relevant data being persons aged between 13 and 17 years of age. For example, the number of persons who should have just reached 18 years of age by April 1983 may be taken to be the numbers of persons who were recorded as being 16 years of age in the 1981 census. Deaths in the age groups in question are virtually nil and we feel that the effect of migration may also be taken as negligible. Indeed the net effect of migration of the whole 15 to 19 year age group between 1979 and 1981 was an outflow of only 6,400 persons and much of this must be amongst persons aged 18 and 19 years of age. As mentioned in chapter 2, deaths amongst those aged 18 years and over amount to about 96 per cent of all deaths. Hence we know, approximately, the sizes of the two terms defining the natural increase amongst Entitled Electors. Thus if the expected natural increase in this group in a given year is subtracted from the change which we have estimated to have actually occurred the result is the net effect of migration, i.e., migration amongst persons aged 18 years and over. Now as the Entitled Elector series stands it represents the relevant numbers in September of each year. As in the second section of the chapter we would like to transform this series to represent April figures. This is esily done. We have already proposed an appropriate adjustment in the form of equation (4.1) earlier in the chapter and we have also seen that with the parameter γ set to ¼ we obtain the series which gives the greatest correlation with the April dated census data. Thus an estimate of the flow of Entitled Electors between April of year $t-1$ and April of year t is given by:

$$\Delta G_{it+1} = \Delta E_{it+1} - 1/4 \Delta^2 E_{it+1}$$

Details of all the above mentioned calculations are given in Table 4.7.

According to these figures, there appears to have been net immigration over the first two years of the period, but lately, during 1984, 1985 and 1986, net emigration has occurred. This accords with the way in which the current high level of unemployment arose. During the start of the period the level of unemployment rose rapidly, indicating that few of those who became unemployed or who could not obtain employment exercised the option to migrate. More recently the rate at which unemployment is rising has slowed down, which suggests that many of those who would otherwise be registered as unemployed have left the State. Indeed, by restricting our attention to persons who are 18 years or over we have created a variable which must correspond to migration amongst members of the labour force more faithfully than estimates of migration as a whole. In this sense, column (5) of Table 4.7 represents an important economic variable in its own right.

We can tentatively make estimates of total populations using these figures.

Table 4.7: *Details of the components of the changes in the numbers of Entitled Electors 1981 to 1986*

Year of flow (April to April)	(1)	(2)	(3)	(4) (2) − (3)	(5) (1) − (4)
			'000		
81/82	43.7	66.9	32.1	34.8	8.9
82/83	43.3	68.2	30.8	37.4	5.9
83/84	30.7	67.6	31.2	36.4	- 5.7
84/85	21.3	67.7	31.6	36.1	-14.8
85/86	9.5	67.1	31.6	35.5	-26.0

(1) Changes in the numbers of Entitled Electors (April to April).
(2) Numbers of persons expected to reach 18 years of age by year end.
(3) Numbers of deaths amongst persons aged 18 years and over.
(4) Expected natural increase of Entitled Electors.
(5) Implied net migration of persons aged 18 years and over.

We can use the migration series in the table together with the published figures for births and deaths to update the 1981 census figure in the usual way: for each year we add births, subtract deaths and add net migration. Of course this effectively embodies the assumption that net migration amongst those aged under 18 years was zero across the period in question. These figures are given in Table 4.8.

Table 4.8: *Estimates of population for the years 1982 to 1986 based on estimates of migration for those aged 18 years and over, along with the official population and migration estimates for these years.*

Year (ending April)	Population Estimate	Natural Increase	Migration of persons aged 18 years and over	Official Estimates Population	Official Estimates Migration
			'000		
1981	3443.4	—	—	—	—
1982	3490.5	38.2	8.9	3483	1.8
1983	3534.9	38.5	5.9	3508	-13.5
1984	3562.8	33.6	- 5.7	3535	- 6.6
1985	3578.4	30.8	-14.8	3552	-13.8
1986	3583.6	30.8*	-26.0	—	—

*Assuming the same natural increase as in 1984/1985.

This table also presents the official estimates of population and net migration for the period 1982-85. In general, our migration estimates show immigration of about 14,800 in the years 1982-1983 while the official figures show emigration of 11,700 in this period. Both sets of data show appreciable emigration in 1984 and 1985.

Conclusion

This chapter showed that the Entitled Elector series developed in chapter 3 may be used, through the ratio-correlation method, to make regional estimates of past population levels, and that the migration series implicit in these estimates behaves in a more realistic manner than that presented in Whelan and Keogh (1980). The model also embodies ideas proposed by Hughes (1981) and attempts to allow for the affect of shiftng age structures over time, to which the ratio-correlation method is sensitive. The data generated in this way are of historical interest and may be used as basic data for other studies.

It was also shown that the new Entitled Elector series may be used in a different way to make estimates of recent population levels for the State as a whole. With this approach the population in 1986 was estimated to be in the region of 3,584,000 persons.

Chapter 5

THE ELECTORAL REGISTER AS A SAMPLING FRAME

Introduction

An initial requirement for any survey is a sampling frame, i.e., a list, map or other device which can be used to locate members of the target population. Many studies are based on lists drawn up for administrative purposes, lists of firms, membership lists, etc. In drawing samples of the general population (at the individual or household level) the following approaches are in common use in Ireland[26].

(a) *Quota Samples:* this is the type of sample commonly used in market research. Its essential feature is the use of "quota controls", i.e., specifications for each interviewer of the categories of respondent they are to interview. These quota controls ensure that the sample will represent the population in terms of the variables embodied in the controls, for example, in terms of age, sex and social status. Apart from fulfilling the quotas, selection of respondents is left more or less to the interviewer's discretion. Quota samples are quick and relatively inexpensive to carry out. For scientific work, however, they have two major disadvantages. First, even when the quota controls are perfectly fulfilled, an unknown degree of bias still exists in the selection of respondents. Secondly, it is not, in general, possible to calculate genuine standard errors for quota samples since they are not based on any probabilistic mechanism. Thus, while it is useful in certain contexts, quota sampling does not provide an appropriate basis for fully scientific sampling.

(b) *Random sampling based on Census Enumeration Districts:* this is the approach used by the CSO in carrying out the Labour Force and Household Budget Inquiries (see the Reports of these inquiries for details). In many ways it is the ideal method for drawing scientific random samples. However, it is only feasible for the CSO since it requires access to the Census data at a very disaggregated level.

(c) *Random samples based on the Electoral Register:* this is probably the most common approach used to obtain random samples of the general population. It is, therefore, important to examine the suitability of the Register for this purpose.

[26]Area sampling, which is widely used in the USA and elsewhere (see Kish (1965)) is little used in Ireland.

Two major considerations are involved in assessing such suitability: (i) is the frame free from bias? (ii) does it enable one to select samples with relatively low sampling errors? We deal with each of these topics in turn but a brief explanation of the two concepts, bias and sampling error, is appropriate here. When applied to a sampling frame, the term bias means the systematic under- or over-representation of certain sub-groups of the target population. This will lead to errors in the estimates derived from samples based on the frame. These errors will not diminish as the sample size increases; indeed, they would persist even if every element on the frame were enumerated. Sampling errors arise from the nature of the sampling process. Even if a frame is free from bias, random samples based on the frame will yield varying estimates depending on which particular elements were selected. The extent of variation in the estimates around the overall average is the sampling error. Such errors, will, in general, diminish as the sample size increases. They are measured by means of the standard error or confidence interval. Sampling errors are affected by features of the sample design such as stratification, clustering etc. These are considered in the second part of the chapter.

Bias on the Electoral Register

We begin by considering the Register as a frame from which to select samples of Entitled Electors as defined above, and go on to discuss how samples of other populations may be derived from it.

Kish (1965) defines a perfect sampling frame as one in which "every element appears on the list separately once, only once and nothing else appears on the list". Let us now consider each of the types of error listed in Table 2.12 above by reference to this definition.

Category	Estimated Number (per cent)	Comment
A. Unregistered Comers of Age	19,700 (0.9)	Represent a bias on the Register against the younger aged groups, especially 18, 19 and 20 year olds.
B. Undeleted Deceased Persons	19,000 (0.9)	Their presence raises interviewing costs because of fruitless calls by interviewers but they do not cause a bias.

C. Unregistered Immigrants   8,500 (0.4)   Represent a bias on the Register against recent immigrants from abroad.

D. Undeleted Emigrants   9,200 (0.4)   As with B, they raise costs but do not create bias.

E. Unregistered Persons   38,900 (1.8)   Represent a bias against recent movers.

F. Double Registrations   127,900 (5.8)   This group will be over-represented by a factor of two in the lists assigned to interviewers, but, provided interviewers call only to the listed addresses, will be correctly represented in the achieved sample. Hence, they do not constitute a bias.

G. Persons Registered in the wrong place   20,200 (0.9)   Represent a bias in the Register against recent movers.

It can be seen, therefore, that categories A, C, E and G constitute biases of the Register. The total of these comes to some 87,000 or about 3.9 per cent of the total number of Entitled Electors. The groups especially affected by this bias are the young and recent movers. As we saw in the survey results reported in Chapter 2, the latter are likely to be younger, (and hence in the early stages of household formation, and resident in urban areas) and in clerical or professional occupations.

However, the overall extent of the bias for samples of the general population is not large[27]. Furthermore, it should be borne in mind that for the effect of a bias to be serious two conditions must be fulfilled: (i) the number excluded must be substantial; (ii) the persons excluded must differ appreciably from the rest of the population in their answers to the particular question. To show this, let us assume that N_1 persons are listed on the Register and N_2 are excluded.

---

[27]One strategy frequently adopted in the ESRI to reduce the bias against recent movers is to instruct interviewers to call to a listed respondent's new address if it is reasonably close to the old one. This gives persons in Category F slightly more chance of selection than others, but helps to mitigate the bias attributable to Categories E and G.

Further, let $\overline{Y}_1$ be the mean for the N_1 listed persons, $\overline{Y}_2$ the mean for the unlisted persons and $\overline{Y}$ be the overall mean for the total population $(N_1 + N_2)$. Further, let W_1 be the proportion included and W_2 the proportion excluded, i.e.:

$$W_1 = \frac{N_1}{N_1 + N_2} \text{ and } W_2 = \frac{N_2}{N_1 + N_2}$$

Having completed the fieldwork, we have an estimate $\overline{y}_1$ based on a sample from the N_1 listed elements. The error attributable to the bias is:

$$E(y_1) - \overline{Y} = \overline{Y}_1 - \overline{Y} = \overline{Y}_1 - (W_1\overline{Y}_1 + W_2\overline{Y}_2)$$
$$= W_2(\overline{Y}_1 - \overline{Y}_2)$$

The smaller the proportion excluded (W_2) the smaller the bias. Also, if $\overline{Y}_1$ and $\overline{Y}_2$ are not substantially different the effect of the bias will not be serious even if W_2 is relatively large. Hence, only in surveys where the variable of interest is powerfully affected by age or recency of moving will the biases on the Register be important. Examples of such surveys would be studies of household formation or of the attitudes of persons under 25 years. "Linking procedures" as described by Kish (1965), should be consdered in such situations.

Samples of Other Populations
    The above discussion related to selecting samples from the population of "Entitled Electors" i.e. the set of persons who were eligible to be included on the current Register. This does not, of course, correspond exactly with the total population aged 18 years and over at the date of the survey. If the latter is the target population, the following additional biases must be considered:
(a)   persons who never get on to the Register;
(b)   persons who have moved since the last qualifying date (15 September) for inclusion in the Register[28].
(c)   persons who became 18 years in the period between April 15 and the date of survey;
(d)   immigrants who arrived since the last qualifying date.

    For most surveys, it seems unlikely that the under-representation of these groups will have serious effects.
    As well as "named respondent" samples of all adults aged 18 years and over, a variety of other populations can be sampled using the Register. For instance,

[28]If, as is normal practice in the ESRI, interviewers are instructed to call to the named respondent's new address, if it is reasonably close to the old one, the effect of this bias will be reduced.

many studies require samples of households. Of course, one cannot validly make inferences about households directly from a sample of named respondents, since, the probability that a given household is selected, depends on the number of listed electors in that household. Hence, such samples will be biased towards the larger households. Valid samples of households may be selected in two ways:

(i) One may take a large number of persons from the Register and accept only those who are the first listed member of a given household. The disadvantage of this procedure is that one cannot always identify a household from the Register, as surnames are only an approximate guide to households. For instance, a married woman's mother living in the married woman's household cannot be identified as a member of that household because the surnames will be different. Furthermore, in some rural areas the individuals in each townland are listed in alphabetical order and households cannot be identified.

(ii) A sample of persons may be selected from the Register in the usual way and in the course of the interview, the number of persons in each household who are on the Register, or are 18 years or over[29], is ascertained. At the analysis stage, one then applies a weight to each respondent inversely proportional to the number of electors in the household. This method avoids the biases implicit in method (i) but has the disadvantage of making the analysis more complex.

Samples of rare or special populations can be generated by means of a sift. This means using an existing survey to identify members of the special population who can be interviewed for a subsequent inquiry. Examples of this method used in samples selected from the Irish Register include a sample of persons aged 65 years or over and a sample of persons aged 18-24 years who had left fulltime education. In each of these cases, the EEC Consumer Survey, which is based on the RANSAM system described below, provided the basis for the sift. In the course of the fieldwork for the Consumer Survey, households containing members of the target population were identified. These were subsequently re-visited to carry out the special survey. In general, this method is a convenient and cheap way of generating genuine random samples of relatively rare populations from the Register. However, the study of persons aged 18-24 years who had left full time education illustrates clearly the problems which can be caused by bias on the Register. When the results of the achieved sample were compared with detailed Census tabulations, it was found necessary to apply substantial weights to the data to correct for

[29]For sampling purposes this would be adequate as an indication of the number in the household on the Register.

deficiencies of married females in smaller households. These deficiencies arose from the biases in the Register against recent movers and those in the early stages of family formation (see Sexton and Whelan, forthcoming).

Sampling Errors in Samples based on the Register

We now turn to assess the possibilities offered by the Register for reducing the second type of error mentioned in the introduction, i.e. sampling error. We begin by examining the features of the Register on which efficient sample designs can be based. Brief descriptions of two designs in common use follow, and the chapter concludes with some correctly computed standard errors for one of these designs.

Our first task is, then, to examine the possibilities for efficient sample design offered by the Register. Few practical survey samples are simple random samples: most incorporate a variety of features designed to increase precision, reduce costs or facilitate analysis. The feasibility of using any of these devices depends on the sampling frame. Three of the most common such devices are stratification, clustering and equal probability of selection (epsem).

Stratification involves the division of the population into relatively homogeneous sub-groups and the selection within each sub-group of separate random samples. Stratification may be proportionate or disproportionate. Since the Irish Electoral Register includes only two characteristics of each elector, viz. sex and address, these are the only variables by which it is possible to stratify single stage samples drawn from it. Electors are listed on the Register in address order, so that stratification by county and county borough is relatively straightforward. However, such strata do not correspond to an urban/rural stratification of the population since most counties contain both urban and rural areas. A proper urban/rural stratification would be desirable so as to increase the homogeneity of strata and hence increase the precision of one's estimates. However, such a stratification system has not been devised for the Irish Register and most samples rely on stratification by county only.

These remarks apply only to single stage samples. Many of the sample designs used in practice involve two or more stages of selection. One could, for instance, take a sample of District Electoral Divisions (DEDs), within each DED a sample of households and within households a sample of persons. The DEDs are then referred to as Primary Sampling Units (PSUs), the households as second stage sampling units and the persons as third or final stage sampling units.

In using the Register to generate multi-stage sample designs, the possibilities for stratification are greatly increased. The Census of Population provides detailed information for DEDs on a large number of variables such as sex, occupation, age, housing conditions, etc. By identifying each polling district with a DED, and using the polling districts of the Register as a primary stage unit (PSU), it is possible to utilise the Census data to stratify these PSUs. Alternatively, the DEDs can be used as primary stage units as described below in relation to the Joint National Media Research (JNMR) design.

Clustering is a technique which also involves dividing the population to be sampled into sub-groups. However, only some of the sub-groups are sampled. Frequently, two or more stages of selection are involved. Unlike stratification, clustering usually reduces the precision of one's estimates. Its value lies mainly in the cost reductions which it makes possible, especially when one is sampling scattered populations in rural areas.

In sampling from the Irish Register, it is customary to use as clusters either the polling districts of the Register or DEDs as shown in the Census. However, it is desirable to ensure that clusters do not vary too much in size, hence small contiguous polling districts or DEDs are sometimes combined to form suitable clusters. For example, when using the Polling Districts of the Register as PSUs, a minimum cluster size of about 400-500 is specified together with a sampling fraction of between 0.01 and 0.15. The resulting samples from each cluster are convenient interviewer workloads.

Th analysis of survey data is considerably facilitated if one's sampling method is an epsem one. This means that the sample is self-weighting and re-weighting during analysis is not required. Such a feature is incorporated in the RANSAM system described below.

Sample Designs based on the Register

This section briefly reviews two sample designs which have been used to generate national random samples: that employed in the Joint National Media Research 1972-1983 (Irish Marketing Surveys 1972-1983) and the RANSAM system developed at ESRI (see Whelan 1979).

The JNMR study used urban districts, DEDs (Wards) or amalgamations of these as primary sampling units. These PSU's were stratified by region and area type (county boroughs, other urban areas and rural areas) and within Dublin a dichotomisation between areas of high rateable valuation and low valuation was employed. This yielded the following 12 strata:

1. *Dublin 1*   Dun Laoghaire and residential wards in Dublin County Borough for which the ratio of the number of private dwellings with a valuation of £27 or more to total population exceeds 0.03.
2. *Dublin 2*   Other Wards in Dublin County Borough.
3. *Dublin 3*   The remainder of County Dublin.
4. *Rest of Leinster 1*   Towns with 1,500 or more population in Leinster (excluding County Dublin).
5. *Rest of Leinster 2*   The remainder of Leinster (excluding County Dublin).

6. *Munster 1*	The County Boroughs of Cork, Limerick, Waterford and the rural district of Cork.
7. *Munster 2*	Other urban towns in excess of 1,500 population in Munster.
8. *Munster 3*	The remainder of Munster.
9. *Connaught 1*	Towns with 1,500 or more population in Connaught.
10. *Connaught 2*	The remainder of Connaught.
11. *Ulster 1*	Towns with 1,500 or more population in Cavan, Donegal and Monaghan.
12. *Ulster 2*	The remainder of Counties Cavan, Donegal and Monaghan.

The published description does not disclose the total number of PSU's or their average size.

Within each stratum, the wards, district electoral divisions, or contiguous groupings of DED's were arranged in descending order of population. A cumulative sum of population in each stratum was formed, and a total of 300 sampling points was selected with probability of selection proportionate to the adult population, as adjusted by the over-representation contained in the sample design[30]. Systematic random sampling procedures were used, thus a fixed sampling interval was applied to a random start.

The second stage of the sample involved acquiring the books of the Electoral Register covering each selected PSU. From these, a sample of electors was drawn with equal probability. The selection of these electors was effected by systematic sampling from a random start, thus ensuring geographical scattering within the PSU.

At the third stage of selection, the sample of electors above was used as though it were a sample of households. The interviewer was required to contact any responsible member of the selected elector's household at the address specified on the register, and the person so contacted was asked to complete the contact questionnaire. If the selected elector's total household was no longer resident at the addess specified for him in the register, the interview took place with any member of the household occupying the chosen elector's former dwelling.

During the contact interview, the full household composition of persons aged 15 years and over was enumerated. Relevant personal demographic data on each adult was obtained (irrespective of whether the contact person was ultimately selected as the individual for interview or not). The interviewer then

---

[30]The sample was deliberately designed to over-represent urban areas.

obtained information relating to consumer durables from that person.

Having listed all adults in the household, and also established the number of electors in the household (this latter information being essential for corrective weighting of the samples), all individuals were selected for interview, using the Kish sampling technique, based on address serial number and alphabetical listing of names (see Kish 1965).

The JNMR sample was not an epsem one. Reweighting was required: (a) to adjust for the under-representation of 15-17 year olds; (b) to adjust for deliberate under-representation of rural areas; and (c) to bring the results into concordance with known Census data on region/area type, sex and age.

The RANSAM system, the ESRI's computer-based procedure for generating national and regional random samples is fully described in Whelan (1979). A brief summary together with some comments on improvements since 1979 will be given here. All stages of sampling in this system are based on the Register. The PSU's employed are individual polling districts (or amalgamations of contiguous districts). These are stratified geographically by county and in Dublin by Dail constituency. Since 1979, the system has been improved so that it is now possible to identify the number of electors from each DED within a given polling district. Stratification of PSU's by reference to the Small Area Census Data for the whole country is, therefore, now feasible. Such stratification will, it is hoped, be adopted shortly since the Small Area Data from the 1981 census are now available.

The lack of correspondence between the DED's as used in the Census and the polling districts in which the Register is published poses problems for both sample designs. In the JNMR design, this lack of correspondence makes very difficult the identification of particular polling districts with particular PSU's. In RANSAM, the problem asserts itself in the difficulty of identifying particular PSU's on a map and in deriving data on the PSU's from the Census. It is hoped that, by linking the computer file created for RANSAM with the Small Area Census Data, this problem will be alleviated in the future.

Precision of Samples using RANSAM

We now turn to some calculations of sampling error (precision) based on RANSAM samples from the Electoral Register. It will be recalled that the primary sampling units are books, or amalgamations of books, of the Register. A set of such PSUs is selected with probability proportional to size and a sample of a fixed number of electors is then taken from each PSU. Cochran (1963), shows that the sampling variance for a sample of this type is:

$$v\left(\hat{\bar{\bar{Y}}}_{pps}\right) = \left(1/\left\{n(n-1)m^2\right\}\right)\sum_{1}^{n}(y_1 - \bar{y})^2$$

where n = the number of PSUs in the sample

        m = the (fixed) sample size per PSU

        y_i = the sample total in the i-th PSU

        $\overline{y}$ = the mean per PSU

    = $\Sigma y_i/n$ = the sample total divided by n

This can also be expressed as:

$$v\,(\hat{\overline{Y}}_{pps}) = 1/\{n(n-1)\} \sum_{i}^{n} (\overline{y}_1 - \overline{\overline{y}})^2$$

where $\overline{y}_i$ is the mean in the ith PSU and $\overline{\overline{y}}$ is the overall sample mean.

Data from two comparable surveys were used to provide empirical estimates of precision based on this formula. Both were conducted in January 1981 and utilised a similar questionnaire. They are referred to as the "Test" and "Control" studies. The "Test" employed 26 clusters (PSU's) of approximately 48 respondents each and the "Control", 38 clusters of 32 respondents each[31].

Table 5.1 gives the estimates and 95 per cent confidence intervals for a variety of variables from both surveys. The confidence intervals for the range of variables shown average 3.16 in the Test sample and 2.73 in the Control sample. The range is quite substantial, running from 0.27 to 9.12 per cent.

The column headed "Ratio of Confidence Intervals" gives an idea of the loss in precision through using clusters of 48 rather than 32. The average ratio is about 1.15, indicating a 15 per cent loss in precision. If one had to choose between the test and control sample designs, this loss would have to be balanced against the cost savings achieved by the relatively dense clustering, i.e., shorter distance between sampled households, in the Test sample.

The estimated confidence intervals give some indication of the design effect for RANSAM, i.e., the ratio of the standard errors of typical variables to those which would be achieved if a simple random sample had been used. Such a simple random sample would yield an estimated standard error of

$$s.e. = \sqrt{\frac{p(1\text{-}p)}{n}}$$

where p is the observed proportion in a given category. The 95 per cent confidence interval can be derived as 1.96 (s.e.). Thus, for each value in Table

---

[31]Note that the total sizes of the Test and Control samples are approximately equal.

5.1 a corresponding simple random sample confidence interval can be derived and the ratio of this to the confidence interval shown in the table gives the design effect. Most of the design effects so calculated are in the range 1-2. The mean design effect is 1.74 for the Test sample and 1.60 for the control. A few lie appreciably outside this range, namely, Is the Head of Household (HOH) a farmer? Is the HOH in the Professional/Managerial category? Did the HOH leave school at Primary? Was the household income unknown or refused? The reason for the poorer precision of these estimates probably arises from high intra-cluster correlations for the items, i.e., from the fact that clusters (PSU's) tend to be homogeneous with respect to these characteristics. It should be noted that improvements in precision could be obtained by increasing the number of clusters or the total sample size or both.

These estimated design effects provide some rationale for the common practice of estimating the standard errors of complex sample designs by calculating the standard error for a simple random sample of the same size and multiplying by a factor such as 1.5 or 2.

Conclusions

We have shown that the Electoral Register is the best generally available frame from which samples of the Irish population may be selected. While it does contain some bias against younger people and recent movers, this is unlikely to be serious except where the variable of interest is powerfully affected by age or recency of moving. It was also demonstrated that samples of other populations (households, persons with special characteristics) may be based on the Register.

The standard errors calculated for a variety of variables from a particular study illustrate that an acceptable degree of precision can be achieved from samples based on the Register. For most variables, design effects are in the range 1.5-2.0. However, the standard errors for variables with a high intra-cluster correlation are likely to be high and researchers should exercise particular caution in drawing inferences from such variables.

Table 5.1: Responses to selected questions in the Test and Control Samples, together with the estimated confidence intervals and the ratio of the Test confidence interest to the Control Confidence interval.

QUESTION	TEST		CONTROL		RATIO OF C.I.'s	DESIGN EFFECTS	
	Percentage in Category	Confidence Interval	Percentage in Category	Confidence Interval	(Test/Control)	Test	Control
Is Respondent the Head of Household?							
(1) Yes	40.3	5.19	43.1	4.70	1.104	1.91	1.69
(2) No	59.7	4.32	56.9	3.79	1.139	1.59	1.36
What Sex is Head of Household?							
(1) Male	84.5	3.05	84.6	2.54	1.201	1.52	1.25
(2) Female	15.5	3.53	15.4	2.53	1.395	1.76	1.25
Age of Head of Household							
(1) Under 18	0	0	0.2	0.27	0	—	1.08
(2) 18-29	6.8	2.43	7.9	2.56	0.949	1.74	1.69
(3) 30-39	19.4	5.02	16.0	2.75	1.825	2.29	1.33
(4) 40-49	21.3	2.76	18.7	2.72	1.015	1.22	1.24
(5) 50-59	22.2	2.93	23.5	2.68	1.093	1.27	1.12
(6) 60-65	11.7	2.62	13.7	2.34	1.120	1.47	1.21
(7) 66-67	3.6	0.98	4.4	1.13	0.867	0.95	0.98
(8) Over 67	14.3	3.84	14.9	2.91	1.326	1.98	1.45
(9) Don't know	0.8	0.67	0.6	0.52	1.288	1.38	1.20
Employment Status of HOH							
(1) Full-time employed	63.0	5.28	64.3	5.09	1.037	1.97	1.89
(2) Part-time employed	2.4	0.86	3.2	1.88	0.457	1.01	1.90
(3) Unemployed presently	9.2	3.29	8.2	2.21	1.489	2.05	1.43
(4) Living on pension or investment income	21.8	4.67	22.0	3.40	1.373	2.04	1.46
(5) In full-time training or education	0.2	0.22	0.2	0.43	0.512	0.89	1.71
(6) Other	1.3	0.89	2.2	1.33	0.669	1.42	1.61

Table 5.1 (continued)

QUESTION	TEST		CONTROL		RATIO OF C.I.'s	DESIGN EFFECT	
	Percentage in Category	Confidence Interval	Percentage in Category	Confidence Interval	(Test/Control)	Test	Control
Occupation of HOH							
(1) Self Employed (other than Farming)	11.3	1.92	10.6	2.51	0.757	1.09	1.45
(2) Farming (Self Employed)	13.6	7.57	23.5	8.64	0.876	3.98	3.63
(3) Professional and/or Managerial	13.8	6.12	11.3	4.34	1.410	3.20	2.44
(4) Other Non-Manual Workers	17.0	4.10	12.4	3.17	1.293	1.97	1.71
(5) Skilled Manual Workers	22.5	4.58	16.7	3.48	1.316	1.98	1.66
(6) Other Manual Workers	21.0	5.73	22.8	4.71	1.216	2.54	2.00
(9) Don't Know or Not Applicable	0.8	0.66	2.7	1.65	0.400	1.34	1.81
Level of Education of HOH							
(1) Primary Level	54.3	9.12	60.1	8.13	1.122	3.30	2.95
(2) Group Certificate	10.8	2.41	6.1	2.04	1.181	1.40	1.52
(3) Inter Cert	8.3	2.43	9.0	2.48	0.979	1.59	1.54
(4) Leaving Cert	13.6	4.61	13.3	4.27	1.079	2.42	2.24
(5) Other Second Level	2.1	1.18	2.7	1.52	0.776	1.48	1.67
(6) Third Level	9.0	3.79	7.0	2.17	1.746	2.39	1.67
(9) Don't Know	1.9	1.35	1.6	0.92	1.467	1.78	1.30

Table 5.1 (continued)

QUESTION	TEST		CONTROL		RATIO OF C.I.'s	DESIGN EFFECT	
	Percentage in Category	Confidence Interval	Percentage in Category	Confidence Interval	(Test/Control)	Test	Control
What is the total household net income from all sources including bonuses and overtime and from rents, pensions dividends, interest, etc., after deductions for income tax, national insurance etc.?							
£ per week.							
(1) 0- 20	0.1	0.16	0.6	0.46	0.348	0.91	1.06
(2) 21- 40	5.4	1.82	5.7	2.08	0.875	1.45	1.60
(3) 41- 60	9.1	3.16	7.6	1.70	1.858	1.98	1.14
(4) 61- 80	9.1	2.11	7.7	2.33	0.905	1.32	1.55
(5) 81-100	11.4	3.25	8.0	1.76	1.847	1.84	1.15
(6) 101-120	6.7	2.06	6.7	1.99	1.035	1.49	1.42
(7) 121-140	4.6	1.84	4.2	1.62	1.136	1.58	1.44
(8) 141-160	3.4	1.23	2.4	1.03	1.194	1.22	1.20
(9) 161-180	2.8	1.20	2.3	0.98	1.225	1.31	1.16
(10) 181-200	2.9	1.27	2.1	1.40	0.907	1.36	1.74
(11) 200 +	11.7	5.17	7.4	3.17	1.631	2.90	2.15
(12) Non response	6.8	3.01	12.6	5.69	0.595	2.16	3.05
(13) Don't know	26.2	7.63	32.7	6.33	1.205	3.13	2.40

Chapter 6

SOME COMMENTS ON THE USE OF THE REGISTER FOR ELECTORAL PURPOSES

Introduction

The uses of the Electoral Register which have occupied us so far are, of course, quite incidental to its main purpose which is the conduct of elections. In this chapter, we examine briefly the implications for elections of the errors whose magnitude was estimated in Table 2.12 above. Our discussion will draw heavily on the Report of the Working Party on the Register of Electors which was published in March 1983. We also comment on the desirability and cost of improving the Register.

Errors on the Register and Elections

As the Working Party points out, a clear distinction must be drawn between errors which arise from failure to operate the present system of registration satisfactorily and possible inadequacies in the system itself. Frequently, complaints about "inaccuracies" on the Register result from misunderstanding about the nature of the eligibility conditions and the registration process rather than from genuine errors. The Working Party considered both types of problem and concluded that the system as a whole was appropriate but that some improvements in its operation could be made, notably in shortening the delay between the qualifying date and the publication of the Register and in avoiding double printing of Registers.

We accept the Working Party's arguments in favour of retaining the basics of the present system. We will, therefore, concentrate on the "genuine" errors. Such errors break down into two fundamental categories: the exclusion of Entitled Electors; and the inclusion of persons not so entitled. It was shown in Table 2.12 that about 67,000 persons (3 per cent of the Entitled Electors) should have votes but do not, while some 156,000 (7 per cent of the Entitled Electors) are registered who should not be (including those registered twice). It is clear that there are quite different pressures on the registration authorities in relation to the two types of error. Excluded persons are likely to complain strongly either directly or through the political parties while few complaints will be received from those who are registered but are not entitled to be. However, if large numbers of the latter group are left on the Register, the possibilities for electoral abuse in the form of impersonation and double voting are substantially increased. This is clearly most undesirable.

It is difficult for the authorities to reduce both types of error simultaneously, especially given the generally poor level of participation by the public in the registration process. If they try too hard to ensure that nobody is wrongly disenfranchised, they run the risk of leaving too much deadwood on the Register. Conversely, if they assiduously attempt to eliminate all wrongly registered individuals they are in danger of disenfranchising some properly Entitled Electors. The serious problems of deadwood on the Dublin Register since 1979 which were discussed above illustrate clearly the dangers in over-emphasising the avoidance of wrongly disenfranchising electors. In our view, both types of error are undesirable and the authorities should attempt to avoid both.

Improvements in the Compilation of the Register

The Working Party considered the use in compiling the Register of an approach similar to that employed for the Census fieldwork, as well as the possibility of linking the Census and the Register directly. They rejected both suggestions, the first on grounds of cost and second because of the likelihood of detrimental effects on both the Census and the Register from such linking. We would agree that it is not desirable to link the Census and the Register directly. However, it is unfortunate that the Working Party's terms of reference did not cover the value of the Register as a research tool. If it had, they could have commented on the desirability of devoting extra resources to the fieldwork involved in compiling the Register so as to improve its usefulness both electorally and from a research point of view. Such fieldwork would not be as onerous as that of a Census since the information sought is extremely simple. The pay-off from such improvements could be considerable. For example, if the Register were sufficiently accurate, it might be possible to make do with censuses at less frequent intervals than the current norm of five years. The funds so released could be balanced against the additional costs of improving the fieldwork for the Register. Any of the detailed information normally collected in a Census could be obtained by sample surveys such as the Labour Force Survey. Furthermore, such a system would yield an accurate annual population estimate containing valuable information on population flows both internal and external. It is also true, of course, that any improvements effected in the accuracy of the Register by more careful fieldwork would also be desirable from an electoral point of view.

A number of countries (Denmark, Germany and Austria for example) keep registers of their populations. As well as their administrative functions such registers can be used for the purposes of population estimation and sampling. In Britain, the cancellation of the 1976 Census of Population caused a number of local authorities to consider using an "enhanced" electoral register to monitor changes in the size and distribution of the population in their areas. Black (1985) describes in detail the experience with this technique in the area administered by the Strathclyde Regional Council. At the time of the electoral canvass, an interview is carried out with each household to ascertain the ages and sexes of all members. Black shows that useful estimates of population change can be obtained at reasonable cost by using this method. The procedure has also had a beneficial effect on the quality of the Electoral Register.

We would now like to spell out some of the ways in which the Irish Electoral Register could be improved. In the first place, we suggest that the claim form be re-designed so as to obtain some additional information. The reason for each new addition at any address could be obtained so as to distinguish between those who have come of age and movers. Since about 60 per cent of movers are within a registration authority's own jurisdiction, this information would allow the number of double votes to be substantially reduced within the area. A more comprehensive system for exchanging information about movers between authorities should also be introduced since this would allow the number of double votes to be reduced even further.

Secondly, registration authorities should publish some data on the gross flows, i.e., total new comers of age, total arrivals onto the Register, total deletions and total deaths. This would make it possible, by cross-checking against the Quarterly Reports on Vital Statistics, to get a very accurate idea of the annual migration flows between areas. Aggregating the data would provide very useful information about gross and net migration into and out of the State. Also it would give the Registration authorities some idea regarding the accuracy of their procedures, the extent of errors, etc.

Thirdly, it should not be very difficult for the authorities to ascertain for each household the number of persons aged 17 years or less on April 15. This would make it possible to compile directly from the Register an annual count of the total population. By studying the degree of concordance between these counts and the Census data, it should be possible to provide very accurate estimates of regional population. There would also be a feed-back effect on the accuracy of the Register since such studies would suggest areas where the Register as compiled was relatively incomplete or contained an undue proportion of deadwood.

If these improvements could be put into effect, the accuracy of population estimates would be considerably improved. It is noteworthy that it has not been possible to base population estimates directly on the Labour Force Surveys despite the large sample size involved and the very carefully designed sampling and weighting techniques used. If the accuracy of the Register could be improved sufficiently, it should be possible to use a weighting system based on it in conjunction with the Labour Force Surveys to derive census type information on an annual basis.

Conclusion

We have, we believe, shown that the Electoral Register is a valuable research tool both for population estimation and sampling. It has certain deficiencies which we have documented but, for most research purposes, these are neither as serious nor as widespread as anecdotal evidence might suggest. The most important deficiency appears to be the Dublin stockpile. In our view, it is important that this problem is rectified not only for research purposes but more importantly because of the potential for electoral abuse which it involves.

Our paper suggests certain reforms in the way in which the Register is compiled which would greatly enhance its usefulness for reserch purposes. Of course, these reforms would involve some increase in cost but this would be more than re-paid if, as we believe is possible, the reformed Register could permit the Census to be conducted on a ten-year rather than the current five-year basis.

REFERENCES

BLACK, ROBERT W., 1985, "Instead of the 1985 Census: The potential contribution of enhanced electoral registers", *Journal of the Royal Statistical Society (Series A)*. Vol. 148, No. 4.

BLACKWELL, JOHN and JOHN McGREGOR, 1982, *Population and Labour Force Projections by County and Region, 1979-1991*, National Economic and Social Council Report, No. 63.

CENTRAL STATISTICS OFFICE, *Censuses of Population 1956-81*. Dublin, Stationery Office.

CENTRAL STATISTICS OFFICE, *Quarterly Report on Births, Deaths and Marriages, 1980-82*, Dublin, Stationery Office.

CENTRAL STATISTICS OFFICE, *Statistical Abstract 1956-1982*, Dublin, Stationery Office.

CENTRAL STATISTICS OFFICE, *Labour Force Surveys 1976-84*, Dublin, Stationery Office.

CENTRAL STATISTICS OFFICE, *Household Budget Survey 1980*, Dublin, Stationery Office.

COCHRAN, W., 1963, *Sampling Techniques*, Wiley, New York.

ELECTORAL ACTS 1923-63, Dublin, Stationery Office.

DEVIS, T., 1983, "People changing their address: 1971 and 1981". *Population Trends*, Vol. 32, Summer.

HUGHES, J. G., 1980, "What Went Wrong with Ireland's Recent Post-censal Population estimates". *The Economic and Social Review*, Vol. 12, No. 2.

HUGHES, J. G., 1981, "The Relationship between Alternative Population and Migration Series: A Comment": *The Economic and Social Review*, Vol. 12, No. 2.

HUGHES, J. G., and WALSH, B. M. 1980, *Internal Migration in Ireland and their determinants*, Dublin, The Economic and Social Research Institute, paper No. 98.

JOINT NATIONAL MEDIA RESEARCH SURVEY, 1983. Irish Marketing Surveys.

KEATING, WILLIAM, 1976, "An Analysis of Recent Demographic Trends with Population Projections for the years 1981 and 1986", *Journal of the Statistical and Social Inquiry Society of Ireland*, Vol. 22.

KEENAN, J. G., 1981, "Irish Migration, All or Nothing Resolved?" *The Economic and Social Review*, Vol. 12, No. 3.

KENDALL, M. and A. STUART, 1967. *The Advanced Theory of Statistics*, Vol. II. Griffen, London.

KISH, L., 1965, *Survey Sampling*, John Wiley and Sons Inc., New York.

KNAGGS, J. F. and T. KEANE, 1971. "Population Projections". *Journal of the Statistical and Social Inquiry Society of Ireland*, Vol. 22, No. 4.

MacGREIL, 1977. *Prejudice and Tolerance in Ireland*, Research Section, College of Industrial Relations, Dublin.

NAMBOODIRI, N. KRISHNAN, 1972. "On the Ratio-Correlation and Related Methods of Subnational Population Estimation", *Demography*, Vol. 9, No. 3.

O MUIRCHEARTAIGH, C. A. and R. D. WIGGINS, 1977. "Sample Design and Evaluation for an Occupational Mobility Study", *The Economic and Social Review*, Vol. 8, No. 2.

REPORT OF THE WORKING PARTY ON THE REGISTER OF ELECTORS, 1983, Dublin: Stationery Office.

SCHMIDT, PETER, 1976. "A Modification of the Almon Distributed Lag". *Journal of the American Statistical Association*, Vol. 69, No. 347.

SEXTON, J. J. and B. J. WHELAN, 1986, *The Transition from School to Working Life"*, Dublin, The Economic and Social Research Institute, (forthcoming).

SHAW, PAUL R., 1975, *Migration Theory and Fact*. Bibliography Series No. 5 Regional

Science Research Institute, Philadelphia.

TODD, JEAN, and BOB BUTCHER, 1982, *Electoral Registration in 1981,* Office of Population Censuses and Surveys, London.

TODD, J. E. and P. A. DODD, 1982, *The Electoral Registration process in the United Kingdom.* Office of Population Censuses and Surveys, London.

WHELAN, BRENDAN J., 1979. "RANSAM: A Random Sample Design for Ireland". *The Economic and Social Review,* Vol. 10, No. 2.

WHELAN, BRENDAN and GARY KEOGH, 1980, "The Use of the Irish Electoral Register for Population Estimation". *The Economic and Social Review,* Vol. 11, No. 4.

Appendix A

ADJUSTMENT OF THE ELECTORAL REGISTER DATA

A. Of the 868 observations on the Electoral Register (31 counties in 28 years), 3 observations were discarded as outliers after examination of these data plotted against time. These were as follows:

County	Year
Roscommon	1963
Tipperary (N.R.)	1966
Dublin Borough	1977

These data were replaced by the geometric interpolate of the previous and succeeding years for the counties in question.

B. The Borough boundaries of Cork and Waterford were changed during the sample period with the result that earlier and later observations on the Register were not comparable for either the borough or county regions of these counties. The change in Cork took place between 1965 and 1966, that in Waterford between 1979 and 1980.

The following procedure was adopted to adjust for these changes. Since in both cases the boundary of the borough region was extended into the county a fixed proportion 'w' of the county register was added to the borough register for years prior to the change. The county register was then defined as the residual. Assuming the change took place between years T and T + 1 and letting B_t and C_t denote the borough and county registers respectively in year t the adjusted registers $\hat{B}_t$ and $\hat{C}_t$ were defined as:

$$\left. \begin{array}{l} \hat{B}_t = B_t + wC_t \\ \\ \hat{C}_t = (1 - w)C_t \end{array} \right\} \text{for } t = 1, \ldots T$$

To determine w uniquely the condition:

$$\hat{B}_T/\hat{C}_T = B_{T+1}/C_{T+1} \text{ was imposed}$$

i.e. that the relative size of the adjusted Registers in the year before the change was the same as that in the year after the change. Solving for w yields:

$$w = \left(\frac{B_{T+1}}{B_{T+1} + C_{t+1}}\right) - \left(\frac{C_{T+1}}{C_T}\right) \cdot \left(\frac{B_T}{B_{T+1} + C_{T+1}}\right)$$

In the case of Cork in 1965-1966:

$$w = 0.14027988845$$

In the case of Waterford in 1979-1980:

$$w = 0.08086536891.$$

A similar procedure was then applied to the data on populations, births and deaths in these counties for previous years. The same values of 'w' as those used to adjust the Registers were used throughout.

C. Between 1972 and 1973 the age requirement for admission to the Register was lowered from 21 years to 18 years. This resulted in a substantial discontinuity in the Register series of all counties over these years. For this reason an adjustment to all Registers for all years prior to 1973 was required. The Registers for 1973 were also slightly adjusted. The adjustments were made separately for each Register.

Let R_t be the Register of any county in year t. It was supposed that the age limit change took at most 2 years to work itself through, so on the assumption of an otherwise (approximately) constant growth rate in the Register over the years 1972 to 1973:

$$R_{73} = \alpha p^{\gamma} \, R_{72} \text{ and}$$

$$R_{74} = \alpha p^{(1-\gamma)} \, R_{73}$$

where α is the usual growth rate of the register, p is the growth in the register due to the fall in the age limit and γ is a parameter ($0 \leq \gamma \leq 1$) distributing that growth (p) over the relevant 2 years. The parameter α was estimated by the mean growth rate over the surrounding 4 years, 1970-1972 and 1974-1976. Hence:

$$\alpha = \left(\frac{R_{72}}{R_{70}} \cdot \frac{R_{76}}{R_{74}}\right)^{\frac{1}{4}}$$

taking logs yields:

$$\gamma \log p = \log R_{73} - \log R_{72} - \log \alpha$$

$$(1 - \gamma) \log p = \log R_{74} - \log R_{73} - \log \alpha$$

Hence:

$$\log p = \log R_{73} + \log R_{74} - \log R_{72} - \log R_{73} - 2 \log \alpha$$

giving p uniquely. γ was then determined as:

$$\gamma = (\log R_{73} - \log R_{72} - \log \alpha)/\log p$$

using the above equations.

Having derived α, p and γ, the adjusted register for years prior to the change was calculated as the true register inflated by the appropriate amount. In particular if R^*_t denotes the adjusted register in year t then:

$$R_t^* = p R_t \quad \text{for years prior to 1973}$$

$$R_{73}^* = p^{1-\gamma} R_{73} \text{ for 1973.}$$

Thus all registers prior to 1973 were inflated by the total growth due to the age limit change and those of 1973 were inflated by the growth which occurred a year after the age limit change but which was a delayed effect of this change.

D. Finally, it became clear as a result of contacts with the Dublin Borough registration authorities that a change in the manner in which the Register was compiled occurred in 1979. Whereas previously individuals about whom no information could be obtained were deleted from the Register, the new practice is to leave such people on the Register. This procedure was partially introduced in 1979 and fully instated by 1980. The result of this was a lowering of the measured outflow of individuals from the Borough and hence an overall increase in the net changes in the Register in recent years. In particular, the Register was rising at a time when the Borough population was falling as measured in the 1979 and 1981 Censuses.

The effect on the data manifested itself as an upward step in the first differences, yielding two large values in the second differences of the Register. Figures for these series are given below:

Year	Register	1st Difference	2nd Difference
1977	364,889	-2,396	-2,793
1978	362,508	-2,381	15
1979	363,943	1,435	3,816
1980	373,812	9,869	8,434
1981	383,223	9,411	-458
1982	392,765	9,542	131

From this it appears that the annual rate of increase in the Register has gone up by between 8,000 and 10,000 persons, who presumably correspond to an annual flow of people leaving the address at which they are registered and not being deleted.

To remove this effect the second differences for 1979 and 1980 were replaced by the mean second difference over the years 1975-1978, 1981 and 1982, (which was -669) and the series was reintegrated. Hopefully this adjustment removes most of the effect of the change in procedure. The new data are thus:

Year	Register	1st Difference	2nd Difference
1977	364,889	-2,396	-2,793
1978	362,508	-2,381	15
1979	359,458	-3,050	-669
1980	355,739	-3,719	-669
1981	351,562	-4,177	-458
1982	347,516	-4,046	131

It is not easy to provide a hard rule for making further adjustments to Dublin Borough as new Registers become available. The most recently published Registers (1986) show Dublin Borough standing at 389,409 which would indicate that the stockpile is no longer growing as before. However, this figure is still substantially in excess of the adjusted figure of 347,516 (above) for 1982, and still at odds with the census result that the Borough population is falling. For the purposes of making population estimates we constructed forecasts of the Entitled Electors in the Borough for the years 1982 to 1986 using equation (3.10) of chapter 3. These were used when we made our population estimates for those years.

Appendix B

1. What is time schedule for compiling the Register?

   _____
   _____
   _____

2. Who compiles it?

   _____
   _____
   _____

3. How are new voters captured ((a) those who come of age, (b) recent movers)?

   _____
   _____
   _____

4. How are dead voters deleted?

   _____
   _____
   _____

5. How are voters who have moved deleted?

   _____
   _____
   _____

6. What steps do you take to avoid double registration (in your own area or in others)?

   _____
   _____
   _____

7. Is every household canvassed?

   _____
   _____
   _____

8.   How many objections are there to the draft register?

_____

_____

_____

9.   Who objects?

_____

_____

_____

10.   Do elections have any effect on the Register?

_____

_____

_____

11.   Have there been any changes in procedure since 1960?

_____

_____

_____

12.   Is the Register for your county/county boro' computerised?

_____

_____

_____

13.   if yes, in what way? (machine, format etc.)

_____

_____

_____

14.   Is it possible to get maps of the polling districts?

_____

_____

_____

Questionnaire for the Field Surveys

ESRI SURVEY OF CHANGES OF ADDRESS

Name _____   County

Address _____   Cluster

_____   Person

County | 1-2
Cluster | 3-4
Person | 5

If data cannot be obtained, either from respondent or from other household member, code the reason why below and return blank questionnaire:

Respondent too ill to respond 1

Respondent moved away permanently.................. 2

Respondent away temporarily (in hospital, on holidays etc.) 3

Respondent deceased................................. 4

Information refused................................. 5

Cannot locate address/building demolished.............. 6

Other (specify)..................................... 7

6

The Economic and Social Research Institute is conducting a study of people who have recently changed address. We want to find out how and why people move house so as to improve our estimates of the country's population. We have selected a random sample of people from the Electoral Register and we very much hope you will be able to help us. Of course, everything you tell us will be treated in the strictest confidence and will only be used to make statistical tables. The interview will not take more than about 10 minutes.

Month | | 7-8

Q.1   When did the respondent move to this address?

Year | | 9-10

| | 11

(Interviewer: Was this prior to April 1971?)   Yes......1   Go to Q.7
                                                No.......2

Q.2   What was the respondent's previous address? (Exact Address)

_____

_____ | | 12-13

_____

Q.3   How many people moved from the old address with the respondent to this | | 14-15
       address? (Exclude respondent)

Q.4   How many of the people who moved with the respondent are still living here? | | 16-17
       (Exclude respondent)

Q.5   Was the respondent's move to this address due to him (her) or a member of
       the household coming to a new job here or seeking employment here?

| | 18

Yes.......... 1   No............. 2

Q.6   Which member of the respondent's household?
       (Code first that applies)

Respondent   1

Respondent's Spouse   2

Parent....................   3 | | 19

Other.....................   4

Now we would like some basic data about the respondent

Q. 7   Sex   Male................ 1

                                 Female.............. 2   □ 20

                                                                          Day   □ □ 21-22

Q. 8   Date of birth   Month   □ □ 23-24

                                                                          Year   □ □ 25-26

Q. 9   Marital Status   Single.............. 1

                                 Married............. 2

                                 Widowed............. 3

                                 Other............... 4   □ 27

Q. 10   Present Occupation   _____
        (Describe fully. If
        unemployed or   _____
        retired, state this
        and give former   _____   □ □ 28-29
        occupation).

Q. 11   Nationality   Irish............... 1

                                 British............. 2

                                 Other EEC........... 3

                                 Other............... 4   □ 30

Q. 12   Finally we would like to ask you about the people in the household. (Include respondent)

                                                                          (a)   □ □ 31-32
(a)   How many members are there in your present household?
                                                                          (b)   □ □ 33-34
(b)   How many of these were under 18 on 15 April this year?
                                                                          (c)   □ □ 35-36
(c)   How many had their 18th Birthday since 15 April 1981?
                                                                          (d)   □ □ 37-38
(d)   How many had their 20th Birthday since 15 April 1981?
                                                                          (e)   □ □ 39-40
(e)   How old is the youngest member of the household?
                                                                          (f)   □ □ 41-42
(f)   How old is the eldest member of the household?

Q. 13   (Interviewer: Code the following from observation)

(a)   How many households are there in the dwelling?

                        One...............1

                        More than one.......2   □ 43

(b)   What type of dwelling is it?

                        Privately owned house..................... 1

                        Privately owned flat...................... 2

                        Local Authority house..................... 3

                        Local Authority flat...................... 4

                        Other (specify)........................... 5   □ 44

                _____

                                                Questionnaire Code   □ 80
                                                                     1

ESRI SURVEY OF CHANGES OF ADDRESS

Name _____

Address _____

_____

_____

| | County | | | 1-2 |

| | Cluster | | | 3-4 |

| | Person | | 5 |

If data cannot be obtained from anybody code the reason and return
blank questionnaire.

No other person in locality who
could provide information 1

Information refused 2

Cannot locate address/building demolished 3

Other (Specify) 4

| | 6 |

The Economic and Social Research Institute is conducting a study of people
who have recently changed address. We want to find out how and why people
move house so as to improve our estimates of the country's population. We
have selected a random sample of people from the Electoral Register and we
very much hope you will be able to help us. Of course, everything you tell
us will be treated in the strictest confidence and will only be used to make
statistical tables. The interview will not take more than about 10 minutes.

In general, data on the respondent will be obtained from some other party and
only very occasionally from the respondent. Code from whom information obtained.

Respondent 1

Relative at the above address 2

Relative at different address 3

Non-relative at the above address 4

Non-relative at different address 5

Other (Specify) 6

| | 7 |

DETAILS OF THE RESPONDENTS CHANGE OF ADDRESS

Interviewer: Is the respondent deceased?

Yes 1   No 2

Date of death .... Day

Month

Interviewer: If the respondent is deceased, go to Q. 12.

Year

| | | 8-9 |

| | | 10-11 |

| | | 12-13 |

Q. 1   Where is the respondent living at the moment? (As full an address as possible.
        If the same as the contact address write "same" and go to Q. 6.)

_____

_____

_____   [ ][ ]   14-15

Q. 2   When did the respondent move to this new address?   Month   [ ][ ]   16-17

                                                                          Year   [ ][ ]   18-19

        (Interviewer: Was this prior to April 1971)   Yes 1   Go to Q. 6   [ ]   20

                                                        No 2

Q. 3   How many people moved from this address with the respondent to his new
        address (Exclude respondent) ?   [ ][ ]   21-22

Q. 4   How many people who moved from this address with the respondent to his
        new address are still living there?   [ ][ ]   23-24

Q. 5   What was the respondent's main reason for moving ? (Describe fully)

_____

_____   [ ]   25

_____

                                                                    [ ]   26

DETAILS OF THE RESPONDENT

Q. 6   Sex   Male 1
                    Female 2   [ ]   27

Q. 7   Age ....   [ ][ ]   28-29,

Q. 8   Marital Status   Single 1
                          Married........2
                          Widowed 3
                          Other......... 4   [ ]   30

Q. 9   Present Occupation (Describe fully. If unemployed or retired state this and give former occupation)

31-32

Q. 10   Nationality   Irish....................1

British...................2

Other EEC 3

Other...................4

33

DETAILS OF RESPONDENTS HOUSEHOLD

Q. 11   (a)   How many members are in the respondents household (Include respondent)

34-35

      (b)   How many of these would have been under 18 on 15 April this year.

36-37

Q. 12   (Interviewer: Code from observation)

      (a)   How many households are at the contact address

One 1

More than one 2

38

      (b)   What type of dwelling is it?

Privately owned house 1

Privately owned flat.................... 2

Local Authority house................... 3

Local Authority flat.................... 4

Other (Specify) _____ 5

39

40-79= Blank

Questionnaire Code........   2   80

REGISTER OF ELECTORS

The register of electors for the year beginning the 15th April next is now being prepared. Please help to ensure that the register will be accurate by completing and returning this form NOW. No stamp is required. Please read the notes overleaf.

REMEMBER YOU CANNOT VOTE UNLESS YOUR NAME IS ON THE REGISTER

Section A. CLAIMS to have names included in Register of Electors

Full Postal Address of Residence...
....
....

The following persons aged **18 years or over** (or who will be 18 years of age by 15th April next) were ordinarily resident at the above address on 15th September last:—

SURNAME	OTHER NAME(S)	IS HE OR SHE A CITIZEN OF IRELAND? ("YES" or "NO")
....	....	....
....	....	....
....	....	....
....	....	....
....	....	....

Does any other family or person aged 18 years or over reside at above address? ("Yes" or "No")..............

(The purpose of this question is to ensure that no eligible person is omitted from the Register.)

Section B. CORRECTIONS to draft Register of Electors

If you wish to have any correction made in the Draft Register of Electors (or List of Claims) give details below.

....
....
....
....

I believe the information I give above to be true.

Signature..

Postal Address...   Date....................

No
Stamp
Required

———— FOLD HERE ————

———— FOLD HERE AND INSERT FLAP ————

———— FOLD HERE FIRST ————

NOTES

Please read these notes, complete and sign the form overleaf and post it now.

WHO IS ENTITLED TO BE REGISTERED?

A person is entitled to be registered as a Dáil *and* local government elector if he

(1) is a citizen of Ireland,

(2) will be 18 years or over on 15th April next, and

(3) is ordinarily resident in the State.

A person who fulfils conditions (2) and (3) only, is entitled to be registered as a local government elector.

WHAT YOU SHOULD DO:

Please enter in Section A overleaf the name of every person who ordinarily lives at your address and who is already over 18 years of age or will reach the age of 18 on or before 15th April next. **Include** persons who are temporarily absent, for example, on holiday or as short-stay patients in hospital. **Exclude** any person living temporarily at your address, for example, short-stay visitors. **Exclude** members of the Garda Síochána or the Defence Forces—a special form is available for use by them.

When you have completed this form, post it immediately to the Secretary of the County Council or the City Manager of the County Borough for the area concerned.

CORRECTIONS IN THE DRAFT REGISTER

The draft register is published on 1st December and may be seen at post offices, libraries, garda stations and local authority offices. A list of the claims made for corrections in the draft register is published on 23rd January and may be inspected at the same places. Claims for corrections in the draft register should be made before 15th January and in the list of claims before 30th January. You may use this form to make claims for corrections in the draft register or list of claims. If a name is to be added use Section A. If a name is to be deleted or if any other correction is to be made use Section B. If you desire any assistance or advice about registration as an elector, enquire at the offices of your local county council, county borough council or urban district council or from the County Registrar.

**YOU CANNOT VOTE UNLESS YOUR NAME IS
ON THE REGISTER**

(1042)127313. 400,000. 3-81. F.P.—G20.

APPENDIX E

Adjusted Electoral Register, 1955-1982

County	1955	1956	1957	1958	1959	1960	1961	1962	1963	1964	1965	1966	1967	1968
CORK BOROUGH	77,095	76,393	75,830	74,859	73,969	74,163	74,193	74,239	73,781	74,354	74,978	75,748	76,233	77,050
DUBLIN BOROUGH	355,185	351,031	349,076	343,606	340,779	340,305	339,969	343,559	345,870	344,771	347,014	350,091	353,296	354,166
LIMERICK BOROUGH	31,110	30,712	30,718	30,446	30,180	30,270	30,735	31,402	31,556	33,095	33,438	33,951	33,969	34,131
WATERFORD BOROUGH	20,716	20,694	20,350	20,447	20,293	20,349	20,608	20,880	21,027	21,211	21,510	21,685	21,989	22,058
CARLOW	21,847	21,596	21,483	21,154	20,964	20,958	20,847	20,594	20,558	21,002	21,506	21,392	21,392	21,369
CAVAN	44,066	42,976	42,104	41,271	40,436	40,035	39,412	38,993	38,317	37,999	37,705	37,639	37,598	37,277
CLARE	55,571	54,509	53,785	52,922	52,321	52,025	52,214	51,403	51,460	52,109	52,471	53,132	53,195	53,023
CORK	148,150	146,917	145,494	144,043	142,760	142,483	142,605	142,888	142,499	142,540	144,899	146,387	146,530	146,720
DONEGAL	82,790	81,323	79,881	78,817	77,312	76,544	76,490	76,392	75,775	76,190	75,912	76,218	76,034	75,751
DUBLIN	104,505	108,173	108,446	108,586	109,633	110,665	112,232	115,717	120,033	125,784	133,424	138,273	142,981	148,296
GALWAY	105,624	108,259	101,362	99,813	99,023	98,673	98,786	98,396	98,095	98,290	101,064	100,507	99,855	98,965
KERRY	84,729	83,726	82,756	81,074	80,158	79,005	78,132	76,586	75,914	76,619	77,004	76,556	75,452	75,513
KILDARE	43,053	42,316	42,260	41,640	41,334	41,291	40,969	40,874	40,603	41,511	41,723	42,414	43,012	43,066
KILKENNY	42,904	42,539	42,018	41,312	40,869	40,480	40,181	40,074	39,773	40,236	40,247	40,159	40,148	39,935
LAOIS	32,003	31,442	30,967	30,548	30,241	30,015	29,837	29,473	29,021	29,540	29,574	29,349	29,408	29,291
LEITRIM	27,648	26,874	26,372	25,787	25,109	24,601	24,435	23,922	23,395	22,916	22,684	22,661	22,233	21,942
LIMERICK	60,059	59,472	58,692	57,782	57,047	56,428	56,155	55,674	55,394	55,180	54,806	55,555	55,372	56,191
LONGFORD	22,247	21,922	21,466	20,982	20,630	20,389	20,186	20,019	19,698	19,645	19,463	19,754	19,589	19,480
LOUTH	45,869	45,726	44,927	44,395	44,082	44,433	44,869	45,637	45,511	44,487	44,898	44,929	45,127	45,644
MAYO	94,051	92,455	90,599	88,737	87,213	86,057	85,009	83,143	83,259	80,175	80,612	80,050	78,720	78,018
MEATH	44,534	44,194	43,824	43,031	42,653	42,402	42,064	42,062	42,146	42,721	43,372	44,397	44,634	45,178
MONAGHAN	34,372	33,403	32,629	31,867	31,212	30,931	30,479	30,296	29,845	29,505	30,611	30,231	30,287	30,021
OFFALY	33,947	33,405	33,084	32,548	32,156	32,296	32,363	32,124	32,063	32,142	31,982	32,241	32,281	32,102
ROSCOMMON	44,166	43,291	42,487	41,583	40,691	40,183	39,607	39,128	38,827	38,530	38,412	38,214	37,795	37,154
SLIGO	40,052	39,514	39,027	38,139	37,561	37,486	37,360	36,829	36,087	35,886	35,808	35,180	34,999	34,755
TIPPERARY N.R.	37,950	37,561	36,984	36,555	36,137	35,937	35,933	35,709	35,422	35,886	36,046	36,272	36,498	36,246
TIPPERARY S.R.	48,368	47,723	47,200	46,490	45,704	45,483	45,144	44,676	44,231	45,011	44,673	44,442	44,461	44,578
WATERFORD	29,475	29,252	28,879	28,479	27,987	27,871	27,841	27,606	27,329	27,391	27,419	27,481	27,918	27,649
WESTMEATH	35,961	35,229	35,048	34,357	33,794	33,503	33,428	33,204	32,998	34,061	34,190	33,630	33,776	33,679
WEXFORD	57,136	56,261	55,520	54,782	54,054	53,772	53,347	53,332	53,023	53,281	53,725	54,167	54,384	54,958
WICKLOW	41,306	40,154	40,074	40,298	40,241	39,913	39,619	39,373	39,216	39,372	39,450	40,422	41,093	41,614

Adjusted Electoral Register 1955-1982 *(continued)*

County	1969	1970	1971	1972	1973	1974	1975	1976	1977	1978	1979	1980	1981	1982
CORK BOROUGH	77,828	78,605	79,374	80,557	81,297	82,043	82,394	83,036	83,965	84,610	85,524	86,123	87,095	89,627
DUBLIN BOROUGH	357,957	359,480	361,030	363,592	364,896	366,205	366,888	367,285	364,889	362,508	359,458	355,439	351,562	347,516
LIMERICK BOROUGH	34,113	34,443	34,870	35,682	36,127	36,577	36,719	37,100	37,483	37,643	38,104	38,378	38,798	39,496
WATERFORD BOROUGH	22,311	22,593	22,756	23,053	23,091	23,128	23,036	22,815	22,863	22,951	23,247	23,527	24,164	24,440
CARLOW	21,682	21,791	21,952	22,241	22,517	22,796	23,266	23,462	24,082	24,585	25,014	25,265	25,828	26,848
CAVAN	37,263	37,191	37,219	37,210	37,327	37,445	37,774	37,901	37,900	37,862	38,204	38,403	38,761	39,057
CLARE	53,109	53,437	53,808	54,326	54,852	55,382	55,720	56,614	56,128	56,772	58,138	58,729	59,229	60,902
CORK	147,528	148,244	149,128	151,189	153,124	155,084	157,472	160,000	164,400	165,814	168,793	172,698	175,959	179,536
DONEGAL	75,813	75,877	76,170	76,623	77,081	77,542	77,851	78,639	79,997	81,017	82,458	83,700	85,875	86,986
DUBLIN	157,113	164,290	169,916	178,349	186,827	195,709	206,515	217,086	233,570	244,495	257,453	268,509	282,269	297,387
GALWAY	100,134	100,473	100,657	101,459	102,405	103,360	104,092	106,226	109,214	110,407	112,960	115,358	117,526	122,420
KERRY	76,172	76,205	76,794	78,027	78,942	79,868	80,675	81,728	83,008	83,266	84,495	84,954	85,445	85,723
KILDARE	43,887	44,703	46,281	48,342	49,928	51,567	52,523	54,260	56,343	57,114	59,715	61,768	64,235	68,311
KILKENNY	40,419	40,375	40,623	40,588	40,930	41,275	41,842	42,461	43,293	43,780	44,879	45,716	46,563	47,480
LAOIS	29,468	29,320	29,235	29,376	29,419	29,463	29,346	29,582	30,289	30,946	31,807	32,355	32,895	33,458
LEITRIM	21,493	21,188	21,088	20,855	20,716	20,577	20,362	20,351	20,596	20,599	20,716	20,721	20,691	20,709
LIMERICK	56,459	56,779	57,370	57,537	58,266	59,004	60,091	61,233	61,872	63,598	63,877	64,852	66,637	69,223
LONGFORD	19,377	19,330	19,508	19,859	19,958	20,058	19,800	19,918	20,103	20,311	20,785	20,810	21,158	21,416
LOUTH	46,397	47,194	47,988	48,570	49,388	50,220	50,955	52,169	53,585	54,525	55,299	56,345	57,503	58,867
MAYO	77,460	76,456	76,018	76,067	76,450	76,836	77,146	78,799	80,346	80,716	81,961	82,798	83,472	83,362
MEATH	45,580	46,337	47,040	48,264	49,367	50,495	51,720	53,065	54,590	55,978	57,893	59,443	61,817	63,623
MONAGHAN	30,064	30,088	30,404	30,601	31,080	31,567	32,293	33,028	33,288	33,511	34,126	34,743	34,935	35,501
OFFALY	32,188	32,155	32,320	32,575	32,919	33,266	33,618	34,244	35,076	35,690	36,561	37,147	37,685	38,680
ROSCOMMON	36,891	36,428	36,129	36,867	36,915	36,964	37,041	36,717	37,083	36,786	37,143	37,576	37,722	38,160
SLIGO	34,817	34,402	34,388	34,853	35,031	35,209	35,361	35,467	36,192	36,506	37,369	37,660	38,079	38,975
TIPPERARY N.R.	36,608	36,584	36,527	36,618	36,701	36,783	36,609	37,080	37,877	38,164	38,694	38,887	39,817	40,137
TIPPERARY S.R.	44,935	44,737	44,795	45,135	45,505	45,878	46,379	46,984	47,816	48,161	49,543	50,926	50,796	51,744
WATERFORD	27,930	28,192	28,312	28,788	29,131	29,478	29,984	30,267	31,230	31,754	32,626	33,018	33,614	34,412
WESTMEATH	33,913	34,063	34,200	34,586	34,840	35,096	35,471	35,593	36,595	37,157	38,627	39,095	39,947	40,740
WEXFORD	55,729	55,597	55,739	57,144	57,874	58,614	59,083	60,000	60,691	61,597	63,009	64,045	65,126	66,852
WICKLOW	42,149	42,409	43,001	44,151	45,245	46,367	48,017	49,121	51,177	51,417	53,814	55,192	56,547	58,592

Fitted Entitled Electors 1955-1982

County	1955	1956	1957	1958	1959	1960	1961	1962	1963	1964	1965	1966	1967	1968
CORK BOROUGH	77,095	76,393	75,691	75,115	74,208	73,232	73,344	73,598	73,611	73,202	73,584	74,403	75,170	75,709
DUBLIN BOROUGH	355,185	351,031	346,877	344,524	340,182	336,091	335,781	335,946	338,856	342,275	341,508	342,384	346,057	349,425
LIMERICK BOROUGH	31,110	30,712	30,314	30,082	30,119	29,749	29,632	30,004	30,686	31,215	31,754	33,298	33,282	33,652
WATERFORD BOROUGH	20,716	20,694	20,672	20,493	20,257	20,378	20,243	20,468	20,801	21,016	21,140	21,392	21,669	21,866
CARLOW	21,847	21,596	21,345	21,233	20,924	20,701	20,719	20,637	20,365	20,309	20,792	21,373	21,263	21,165
CAVAN	44,066	42,976	41,886	40,896	40,117	39,296	38,659	38,305	37,700	37,233	36,633	36,449	36,267	36,291
CLARE	55,571	54,509	53,447	52,643	51,895	51,198	50,892	51,040	50,584	50,193	50,911	51,485	52,005	52,283
CORK	148,150	146,917	145,684	144,299	142,810	141,487	141,045	141,318	141,661	141,445	141,244	143,234	145,432	145,646
DONEGAL	82,790	81,323	79,856	78,398	77,107	76,018	74,625	74,397	74,591	74,283	73,859	74,398	74,081	74,421
DUBLIN	104,505	106,173	107,841	109,854	111,095	111,101	112,416	113,749	116,574	121,120	126,509	133,776	140,400	144,316
GALWAY	105,624	103,259	100,894	98,856	97,326	96,399	96,116	96,206	96,089	95,629	95,698	97,827	98,950	97,450
KERRY	84,729	83,726	82,723	81,749	80,151	79,010	78,036	77,085	75,667	74,767	75,498	76,192	75,770	74,570
KILDARE	43,053	42,316	41,579	41,230	41,061	40,447	40,387	40,266	39,987	39,862	40,208	41,081	41,352	42,137
KILKENNY	42,904	42,539	42,174	41,755	41,110	40,426	40,101	39,764	39,566	39,464	39,356	39,951	39,756	39,657
LAOIS	32,003	31,442	30,881	30,388	29,977	29,659	29,442	29,273	28,960	28,483	28,775	29,139	28,856	28,794
LEITRIM	27,648	26,874	26,100	25,553	25,041	24,360	23,804	23,619	23,238	22,637	22,147	21,885	21,881	21,566
LIMERICK	60,059	59,472	58,885	58,211	57,306	56,430	55,807	55,384	55,137	54,675	54,494	54,231	54,307	55,024
LONGFORD	22,247	21,922	21,597	21,215	20,701	20,264	20,007	19,821	19,647	19,426	19,167	19,152	19,130	19,390
LOUTH	45,869	45,726	45,583	44,815	44,153	43,877	44,237	44,787	45,555	45,530	44,388	44,572	44,877	44,999
MAYO	94,051	92,455	90,859	89,164	87,210	85,475	84,216	83,236	81,915	80,507	80,127	77,213	78,563	77,340
MEATH	44,534	44,194	43,854	43,505	43,002	42,159	41,983	41,758	41,482	41,639	41,898	42,691	43,479	44,428
MONAGHAN	34,372	33,403	32,434	31,559	30,856	30,149	29,710	29,472	29,092	28,871	28,383	28,776	29,652	28,984
OFFALY	33,947	33,405	32,863	32,510	32,052	31,593	31,687	31,877	31,667	31,515	31,612	31,516	31,663	31,824
ROSCOMMON	44,166	43,291	42,416	41,579	40,744	39,815	39,131	38,709	38,163	37,809	37,567	37,367	37,263	36,922
SLIGO	40,052	39,514	38,976	38,475	37,713	36,944	36,807	36,825	36,395	35,608	35,237	35,254	34,773	34,337
TIPPERARY N.R.	37,950	37,561	37,172	36,700	36,123	35,750	35,433	35,395	35,362	35,034	35,057	35,648	35,731	35,980
TIPPERARY S.R.	48,368	47,723	47,078	46,501	45,911	45,101	44,607	44,495	44,048	43,553	43,799	44,334	43,709	43,651
WATERFORD	29,475	29,252	29,029	28,745	28,307	27,860	27,488	27,542	27,459	27,134	26,980	27,150	27,179	27,407
WESTMEATH	35,961	35,229	34,497	34,072	33,778	33,000	32,628	32,542	32,451	32,191	32,698	33,633	33,089	32,709
WEXFORD	57,136	56,261	55,386	54,620	53,911	53,182	52,818	52,521	52,396	52,236	52,320	52,857	53,342	53,601
WICKLOW	41,306	40,154	39,002	38,188	38,622	38,876	38,624	38,201	37,935	37,736	37,712	37,966	38,295	39,521

Fitted Entitled Electors 1955-1982 (continued)

County	1969	1970	1971	1972	1973	1974	1975	1976	1977	1978	1979	1980	1981	1982
CORK BOROUGH	76,441	77,286	78,056	78,826	79,970	80,830	81,489	81,877	82,417	83,376	84,102	84,937	85,616	86,494
DUBLIN BOROUGH	350,746	353,487	356,073	357,111	359,496	361,254	362,281	363,079	363,388	361,433	358,426	355,500	351,507	347,388
LIMERICK BOROUGH	33,552	33,692	33,752	34,247	34,867	35,666	35,982	36,307	36,437	36,904	37,196	37,400	37,892	38,159
WATERFORD BOROUGH	22,098	22,179	22,507	22,741	22,929	23,144	23,096	23,069	22,871	22,739	22,896	23,099	23,456	23,905
CARLOW	21,160	21,473	21,634	21,762	22,061	22,357	22,634	23,106	23,331	23,910	24,480	24,890	25,128	25,665
CAVAN	36,130	35,854	35,919	35,873	35,918	35,954	36,115	36,330	36,638	36,637	36,576	36,699	37,106	37,329
CLARE	52,022	51,989	52,322	52,742	53,235	53,795	54,326	54,711	55,426	55,403	55,444	56,912	57,862	58,196
CORK	145,516	146,210	147,087	147,916	149,778	152,010	153,936	156,243	158,841	162,895	165,344	167,319	171,397	175,002
DONEGAL	74,018	73,827	74,018	74,168	74,606	75,120	75,581	75,986	76,418	77,596	79,039	80,091	81,614	83,131
DUBLIN	149,328	156,827	165,778	171,568	178,323	187,639	196,361	206,465	217,725	231,599	246,716	257,104	269,597	281,615
GALWAY	96,607	97,094	98,224	98,237	98,812	99,877	100,868	101,669	103,323	106,423	108,380	110,052	112,854	115,051
KERRY	74,375	75,202	75,421	75,826	77,100	78,178	79,039	79,861	80,864	82,168	82,582	83,502	84,238	84,572
KILDARE	42,397	42,721	43,774	45,022	47,108	49,047	50,518	51,784	52,976	55,149	56,590	58,002	60,851	62,972
KILKENNY	39,605	39,558	40,123	39,980	40,240	40,229	40,715	41,139	41,808	42,521	43,296	43,831	45,142	45,864
LAOIS	28,781	28,854	28,844	28,669	28,777	28,894	28,915	28,832	28,955	29,645	30,423	31,229	31,891	32,359
LEITRIM	21,164	20,771	20,408	20,305	20,139	19,955	19,837	19,634	19,573	19,821	19,919	19,965	20,013	19,964
LIMERICK	54,970	55,887	55,988	56,448	56,942	57,215	58,143	59,041	60,273	61,208	62,162	63,613	63,705	65,285
LONGFORD	19,089	19,002	18,925	18,996	19,327	19,630	19,641	19,586	19,365	19,644	19,863	20,194	20,567	20,574
LOUTH	45,531	46,330	47,168	47,970	48,561	49,330	50,204	50,946	52,120	53,612	54,610	55,307	56,311	57,512
MAYO	75,968	75,552	74,876	73,925	73,881	74,237	74,744	75,102	75,898	78,004	79,062	79,334	80,745	81,369
MEATH	44,438	45,064	45,511	46,394	47,225	48,623	49,685	50,850	52,149	53,593	55,151	56,635	58,656	60,297
MONAGHAN	29,031	28,806	28,943	29,101	29,458	29,751	30,328	30,983	31,743	32,252	32,335	32,735	33,482	33,895
OFFALY	31,630	31,632	31,672	31,783	32,067	32,417	32,782	33,134	33,721	34,582	35,271	36,058	36,740	37,225
ROSCOMMON	36,315	35,804	35,555	35,116	35,420	36,122	35,950	36,015	35,887	35,803	36,036	35,875	36,481	36,786
SLIGO	34,226	34,185	33,983	33,733	34,166	34,548	34,653	34,812	34,924	35,462	36,052	36,654	37,248	37,484
TIPPERARY N.R.	35,995	35,848	36,253	36,080	36,077	36,216	36,296	36,264	36,286	37,126	37,811	38,028	38,493	38,895
TIPPERARY S.R.	43,802	44,084	44,205	43,978	44,273	44,717	45,098	45,543	46,142	46,906	47,536	48,310	50,014	50,551
WATERFORD	27,690	27,392	27,863	28,060	28,274	28,824	29,121	29,534	30,006	30,487	31,515	32,023	32,824	33,127
WESTMEATH	32,938	32,950	33,240	33,357	33,628	34,018	34,232	34,555	34,826	35,360	36,390	37,321	38,514	38,886
WEXFORD	54,056	54,871	54,954	54,840	56,069	57,211	57,797	58,319	59,091	59,926	60,740	62,105	63,326	64,314
WICKLOW	40,028	40,494	40,948	41,206	42,103	43,453	44,534	45,833	47,517	48,708	50,563	50,775	53,692	54,665

Fitted Flows of Entitled Electors 1955-1982

County / Year	1955	1956	1957	1958	1959	1960	1961	1962	1963	1964	1965	1966	1967	1968
CORK BOROUGH	-702	-702	-702	-576	-907	-976	112	254	13	-410	383	819	767	539
DUBLIN BOROUGH	-4,154	-4,154	-4,154	-2,353	-4,342	-4,091	-310	165	2,910	3,420	-767	876	3,673	3,368
LIMERICK BOROUGH	-398	-398	-398	-232	37	-369	-118	372	682	529	539	1,544	-16	371
WATERFORD BOROUGH	-22	-22	-22	-179	-236	121	-135	225	333	215	123	253	277	197
CARLOW	-251	-251	-251	-112	-309	-223	18	-82	-271	-57	483	582	-110	-98
CAVAN	-1,090	-1,090	-1,090	-990	-779	-821	-637	-354	-605	-467	-600	-184	-181	24
CLARE	-1,062	-1,062	-1,062	-804	-748	-697	-305	147	-456	-392	718	574	520	278
CORK	-1,233	-1,233	-1,233	-1,385	-1,489	-1,323	-442	273	342	-216	-201	1,990	2,198	214
DONEGAL	-1,467	-1,467	-1,467	-1,458	-1,292	-1,089	-1,393	-228	194	-308	-424	539	-317	339
DUBLIN	1,668	1,668	1,668	2,013	1,240	6	1,316	1,333	2,825	4,545	5,389	7,268	6,624	3,916
GALWAY	-2,365	-2,365	-2,365	-2,038	-1,531	-927	-283	90	-117	-460	69	2,129	1,123	-1,499
KERRY	-1,003	-1,003	-1,003	-974	-1,599	-1,140	-975	-950	-1,418	-900	731	694	-422	-1,199
KILDARE	-737	-737	-737	-349	-169	-614	-60	-121	-278	-126	346	872	272	785
KILKENNY	-365	-365	-365	-419	-645	-685	-324	-337	-198	-102	-109	595	-195	-99
LAOIS	-561	-561	-561	-493	-411	-318	-217	-169	-313	-477	292	364	-283	-62
LEITRIM	-774	-774	-774	-547	-512	-681	-556	-185	-381	-600	-490	-262	-4	-316
LIMERICK	-587	-587	-587	-674	-905	-876	-622	-423	-247	-462	-181	-263	76	718
LONGFORD	-325	-325	-325	-382	-514	-437	-258	-186	-174	-221	-259	-15	-22	259
LOUTH	-143	-143	-143	-768	-662	-275	359	551	768	-25	-1,142	183	306	122
MAYO	-1,596	-1,596	-1,596	-1,695	-1,954	-1,735	-1,259	-979	-1,321	-1,409	-379	-2,914	1,350	-1,223
MEATH	-340	-340	-340	-349	-503	-843	-176	-225	-276	157	259	793	789	948
MONAGHAN	-969	-969	-969	-875	-703	-706	-439	-238	-380	-222	-487	393	876	-668
OFFALY	-542	-542	-542	-353	-458	-458	93	190	-210	-152	96	-96	148	160
ROSCOMMON	-875	-875	-875	-837	-835	-929	-684	-422	-546	-353	-242	-201	-104	-341
SLIGO	-538	-538	-538	-501	-762	-769	-138	18	-430	-786	-372	17	-482	-436
TIPPERARY N.R.	-389	-389	-389	-472	-577	-373	-318	-37	-33	-328	23	591	83	249
TIPPERARY S.R.	-645	-645	-645	-577	-590	-810	-494	-112	-448	-495	247	534	-624	-58
WATERFORD	-223	-223	-223	-284	-438	-447	-372	54	-83	-326	-154	170	30	227
WESTMEATH	-732	-732	-732	-425	-294	-778	-372	-86	-91	-260	507	936	-545	-380
WEXFORD	-875	-875	-875	-766	-708	-729	-364	-297	-125	-161	85	537	484	259
WICKLOW	-1,152	-1,152	-1,152	-814	434	254	-252	-423	-266	-199	-24	253	329	1,226

Fitted Flows of Entitled Electors 1955-1982 (continued)

County	1069	1970	1971	1972	1973	1974	1975	1976	1977	1978	1979	1980	1981	1982
CORK BOROUGH	732	846	770	770	1,144	860	660	388	539	959	726	835	679	878
DUBLIN BOROUGH	1,321	2,740	2,586	1,038	2,385	1,758	1,027	797	309	-1,954	-3,008	-2,925	-3,993	-4,119
LIMERICK BOROUGH	-100	140	60	495	620	799	316	325	130	467	292	204	492	267
WATERFORD BOROUGH	232	81	328	233	189	215	-49	-26	-198	-132	157	203	357	449
CARLOW	-5	312	161	129	298	296	277	472	224	580	570	412	238	537
CAVAN	-161	-276	65	-46	45	36	161	215	309	-1	-62	124	407	223
CLARE	-261	-32	333	419	493	560	531	385	715	-23	41	1,468	950	334
CORK	-129	694	877	829	1,862	2,232	1,926	2,307	2,598	4,054	2,448	1,975	4,078	3,604
DONEGAL	-408	-191	191	150	438	514	461	405	432	1,179	1,443	1,052	1,523	1,517
DUBLIN	5,011	7,499	8,951	5,791	6,755	9,316	8,722	10,104	11,260	13,875	15,117	10,387	12,493	12,018
GALWAY	-843	487	1,180	12	575	1,065	990	801	1,654	3,100	1,957	1,672	2,802	2,196
KERRY	-195	827	220	404	1,274	1,078	861	822	1,003	1,305	413	921	736	334
KILDARE	260	324	1,053	1,248	2,086	1,938	1,471	1,266	1,192	2,173	1,442	1,411	2,849	2,121
KILKENNY	-52	-47	564	-143	260	-11	486	423	669	713	775	535	1,310	722
LAOIS	-13	78	-10	-174	108	117	21	-83	123	689	778	806	662	469
LEITRIM	-402	-393	-363	-102	-166	-183	-119	-202	-61	247	99	45	48	-49
LIMERICK	-54	917	101	460	494	273	927	898	1,232	935	954	1,451	92	1,580
LONGFORD	-301	-87	-77	70	382	303	11	-55	-221	279	218	331	373	7
LOUTH	532	799	837	802	591	769	874	742	1,174	1,492	998	697	1,004	1,201
MAYO	-1,372	-416	-676	-952	-44	356	507	358	796	2,106	1,058	272	1,411	625
MEATH	10	626	447	883	831	1,397	1,062	1,166	1,298	1,445	1,558	1,484	2,021	1,641
MONAGHAN	47	-225	137	158	357	293	577	605	810	509	83	399	747	413
OFFALY	-194	1	40	111	284	350	365	352	587	860	689	788	682	485
ROSCOMMON	-607	-511	-249	-439	305	701	-171	64	-127	-85	233	-160	606	305
SLIGO	-111	-41	-201	-250	433	382	104	159	112	538	589	602	594	236
TIPPERARY N.R.	15	-147	405	-173	-3	139	80	-32	22	840	685	217	466	402
TIPPERARY S.R.	151	281	121	-227	295	444	381	445	599	764	630	774	1,703	538
WATERFORD	284	-298	471	197	214	550	297	413	472	480	1,028	508	801	303
WESTMEATH	229	12	290	117	272	390	214	323	271	534	1,029	932	1,193	371
WEXFORD	456	814	83	-114	1,229	1,143	586	522	771	835	814	1,365	1,221	988
WICKLOW	506	467	454	257	897	1,350	1,081	1,299	1,684	1,191	1,855	212	2,917	973

ESRI PUBLICATIONS

Books:

Economic Growth in Ireland: The Experience Since 1947
                              Kieran A. Kennedy and Brendan Dowling
Irish Economic Policy: A Review of Major Issues
                    Staff Members of ESRI (eds. B. R. Dowling and J. Durkan)
Irish Economic Policy: A Review of Major Issues
                    Staff Members of ESRI (eds. B. R. Dowling and J. Durkan)
The Irish Economy and Society in the 1980s (Papers presented at ESRI Twenty-first Anniversary Conference)   Staff Members of ESRI
The Economic and Social State of The Nation
                    J. F. Meenan, M. P. Fogarty, J. Kavanagh and L. Ryan
The Irish Economy: Policy and Performance 1972-1981
                              P. Bacon, J. Durkan and J. O'Leary
Employment and Unemployment Policy for Ireland
            Staff Members of ESRI (eds., Denis Conniffe and Kieran A. Kennedy)
Public Social Expenditure — Value for Money? (Papers presented at a Conference, 20 November 1984)
Medium-Term Outlook: 1986-1990. No. 1   Peter Bacon

Policy Research Series:

1. *Regional Policy and the Full-Employment Target*   M. Ross and B. Walsh
2. *Energy Demand in Ireland, Projections and Policy Issues*   S. Scott
3. *Some Issues in the Methodology of Attitude Research*   E. E. Davis *et al.*
4. *Land Drainage Policy in Ireland*   Richard Bruton and Frank J. Convery
5. *Recent Trends in Youth Unemployment*   J. J. Sexton
6. *The Economic Consequence of European Union: A Symposium on Some Policy Aspects*
                    D. Scott, J. Bradley, J. D. FitzGerald and M. Ross

Broadsheet Series:

1. *Dental Services in Ireland*   P. R. Kaim-Caudle
2. *We Can Stop Rising Prices*   M. P. Fogarty
3. *Pharmaceutical Services in Ireland*   P. R. Kaim-Caudle
                    assisted by Annette O'Toole and Kathleen O'Donoghue
4. *Ophthalmic Services in Ireland*   P. R. Kaim-Caudle
                    assisted by Kathleen O'Donoghue and Annette O'Toole
5. *Irish Pensions Schemes, 1969*   P. R. Kaim-Caudle and J. G. Byrne
                    assisted by Annette O'Toole
6. *The Social Science Percentage Nuisance*   R. C. Geary
7. *Poverty in Ireland: Research Priorities*   Brendan M. Walsh
8. *Irish Entrepreneurs Speak for Themselves*   M. P. Fogarty
9. *Marital Desertion in Dublin: An Exploratory Study*   Kathleen O'Higgins
10. *Equalization of Opportunity in Ireland: Statistical Aspects*
                    R. C. Geary and F. S. Ó Muircheartaigh
11. *Public Social Expenditure in Ireland*   Finola Kennedy
12. *Problems in Economic Planning and Policy Formation in Ireland, 1958-1974*
                    Desmond Norton
13. *Crisis in the Cattle Industry*   R. O'Connor and P. Keogh